SKILL SHARPENERS

Third Edition

3

JUDY DeFILIPPO
CHARLES SKIDMORE

Longman

Judy DeFilippo supervises MATESL student teachers at Simmons College in Boston, Massachusetts. She is the author of *Lifeskills 1, 2,* and *3* and co-author of *Grammar Plus.*

Charles Skidmore is the principal of Arlington High School in Arlington, Massachusetts. He has taught and supervised the teaching of English as a Second Language for the past twenty-five years. He also serves as adjunct faculty in the Lynch School of Education at Boston College.

Pearson Education, 10 Bank Street, White Plains, NY 10606

Vice president, primary and secondary editorial: Ed Lamprich
Senior development editor: Virginia Bernard
Vice president, design and production: Rhea Banker
Director of editorial production: Linda Moser
Production supervisor: Melissa Leyva
Associate production editor: Laura Lazzaretti
Marketing managers: Alex Smith/Tania Saiz-Sousa
Senior manufacturing buyer: Dave Dickey
Cover design: Ann France
Cover photo: © Emma Lee/Life File/Getty Images
Text design adaptation: Tracey Munz Cataldo
Text composition: Laserwords
Text font: 11/18 Myriad Roman
Illustrations: Elizabeth Hazelton, Kathleen Todd, Andrew Lange
Photo credits: Library of Congress, pp. 40, 41, 47, 61, 97; Dorling
    Kindersley, p. 52; National Aeronautics and Space
    Administration, pp. 64, 68, 69

ISBN: 0-13-192994-1
Printed in the United States of America
3 4 5 6 7 8 9 10–VHG–14 13 12 11 10 09

Introduction

The *Skill Sharpeners* series has been especially designed for students whose skills in standard English, especially those skills concerned with literacy, require strengthening. It is directed both toward students whose first language is not English and toward those who need additional practice in standard English grammar and vocabulary. By introducing basic skills tied to classroom subjects in a simple, easy-to-understand grammatical framework, the series helps to prepare these students for success in regular ("mainstream") academic subjects. By developing and reinforcing school and life survival skills, it helps build student confidence and self esteem.

Skills Sharpeners focuses on grammar practice and higher order thinking skills. It provides many content-area readings, biographies, opportunities for students to write, and practice in using formats similar to those of many standardized tests. The third edition updates the content of many pages. The central purpose of the series remains the same, however. *Skill Sharpeners* remains dedicated to helping your students sharpen their skills in all facets of English communication.

With English Language Learners, *Skill Sharpeners* supplements and complements any basic ESL text or series. With these students and with others, *Skill Sharpeners* can also be used to reteach and reinforce specific skills with which students are having—or have had—difficulty. In addition, it can be used to review and practice grammatical structures and to reinforce, expand, and enrich students' vocabularies.

The grammatical structures and the language objectives in *Skill Sharpeners* follow a systematic, small-step progression with many opportunities for practice, review, and reinforcement. Vocabulary and skill instruction is presented in the context of situations and concepts that have an immediate impact on students' daily lives. Themes and subject matter are directly related to curriculum areas. Reading and study skills are stressed in many pages, and writing skills are carefully developed, starting with single words and sentences and building gradually to paragraphs and stories in a structured, controlled composition sequence.

Skill Sharpeners is an ideal supplement for literature-based or sheltered English classrooms. *Skill Sharpeners* allows for direct teaching of grammar and language skills that most textbooks and novels do not supply. Students do not always intuitively grasp grammar and language rules. *Skill Sharpeners* has been designed to allow students a vehicle for continued practice in these areas.

Using the *Skill Sharpeners*

Because each page or pair of pages of the *Skill Sharpeners* is independent and self contained, the series lends itself to great flexibility of use. Teachers may pick and choose pages that fit the needs of particular students, or they may use the pages in sequential order. Most pages are self-explanatory, and all are easy to use, either in class or as homework assignments. Annotations at the bottom of each page identify the skill or skills being developed and suggest ways to prepare for, introduce, and present the exercise(s) on the page. In most cases, oral practice of the material is suggested before the student is asked to complete the page in writing. Teacher demonstration and student involvement and participation help build a foundation for completing the page successfully and learning the skill.

Skill Sharpeners is divided into thematic units. The first unit of each book is introductory. In *Skill Sharpeners 1,* this unit provides exercises to help students say and write their names and addresses and to familiarize them with basic classroom language, school deportment, the names of school areas and school personnel, and number names. In later books of the series, the first unit serves both to review some of the material taught in earlier books and to provide orientation to the series for students coming to it for the first time.

At the end of each of the *Skill Sharpeners* books is a review of vocabulary and an end-of-book test of grammatical and reading skills. The test, largely in multiple-choice format, not only assesses learning of the skills but also provides additional practice for other multiple-choice tests.

The Table of Contents in each book identifies the skills developed on each page. An Index at the end of the book provides an alphabetical list of language objectives. The language objectives are also displayed prominently at the top of each page.

Skill Sharpeners invite expansion! We encourage you to use them as a springboard and to add activities and exercises that build on those in the books to fill the needs of your own particular students. Used this way, the *Skill Sharpeners* can significantly help to build the confidence and skills that students need to be successful members of the community and successful achievers in subject-area classrooms.

Contents

Language Objective
Complete sentences with the correct verb form.

Circle the best answer. The first one is done for you.

1. I didn't see you last night. Where | was / (were) | you?

2. Robert can't | find / found | his shoes.

3. Does Kit Ming | takes / take | the bus to school?

4. Everyone | was / were | dancing and singing at the party.

5. I | went / go | to the dentist yesterday.

6. Did you | like / liked | the movie?

7. Jim is | doing / does | his homework now.

8. Are you | rent / renting | an apartment?

9. | Do / Are | you play volleyball?

10. I'm | have / having | a party tonight. Can you come?

11. Ronald likes | ride / riding | his bicycle to school.

12. | Was / Were | Minh in class yesterday?

13. Maria | writes / writing | to her grandmother every month.

14. | Was / Were | the teachers at a meeting yesterday?

15. The bus | leaving / leaves | at ten o'clock.

16. George didn't | washed / wash | the dishes.

SKILL OBJECTIVE: Choosing the correct verb tense and form—simple present and past, present and past progressive. This page may be used as a quick evaluation of the student's ability to distinguish and use the four verb tenses. Do the first example as a group activity, then assign the page as independent work. Students who find the page difficult should be grouped for reteaching. Analyze the type of mistakes being made and provide additional practice in these skills.

Small Talk

A Complete each of these sentences. This first one is done for you.

1. I'm going to the library because   <u>I want to borrow some books.</u>

2. She has to walk to work because _____

3. The concert started late because _____

4. She didn't go to school because _____

5. The girls don't want to go to that movie because _____

6. We are driving to California because _____

7. We stopped at the supermarket because _____

8. We are going to a restaurant because _____

9. David is taking the train to Dallas because _____

B Read the following questions. Answer each question by making a check mark in the right box under *Yes, No,* or *Sometimes.*

	Yes	No	Sometimes
1. Do shirts have buttons?			
2. Do shoes have zippers?			
3. Do pants have sleeves?			
4. Do pants have zippers?			
5. Do men wear blouses?			
6. Do belts go around the chest?			
7. Do hats go on people's heads?			
8. Do shirts have collars?			
9. Do skirts have hems?			
10. Do sweaters have pockets?			

SKILL OBJECTIVES: Reviewing verb tenses; understanding cause and effect; building vocabulary; charting information. Cover Part A as an oral group activity. Students should be as creative as possible and think up as many different reasons as they can for each item. *Part B:* Teach/review clothing vocabulary by giving directions: *If you are wearing a zipper, sit on your desk. If you are wearing more than four buttons, write your name on the board, etc.* Complete the first two items in Part B as a class, then assign the page as independent written work.

2

Likes and Dislikes

Most people like to do some things and do not like to do others. Look at the pictures. Then write what the persons or animals like to do and what they don't like to do. The first one is done for you. Use it as a model for the others.

1. *Samir likes playing baseball, but he doesn't like studying history.*

2. *Carolina*

3. *Binh*

4. *Ed and Al*

5. *My cat*

6. *They*

7. *Elena*

SKILL OBJECTIVE: Using *like(s), doesn't/don't like* plus gerund. Give several statements of likes/dislikes: *I like skiing, but I don't like skating. I like eating, but I don't like gaining weight.* Ask students, "How about you?" After four or five have volunteered, ask their classmates to recall their statements. *Alicia likes playing with babies, but she doesn't like changing them.* If students use the infinitive verb instead of the gerund ("likes to play"), praise the sentence as correct, and encourage students to use both forms for variety. Assign the page for independent written work.

3

Interviewing: Getting To Know Each Other

A Make the following phrases into questions. Ask your classmates the questions. Ask your teacher, too. Try to find one person who can answer "yes." Write the person's name. Be sure to form the questions correctly.

Example: *likes pizza:* "Do you like pizza?"

Name

1. has the same number of brothers and sisters as you do _____

2. is going to celebrate a birthday soon _____

3. wants to have a big family someday (four or more children) _____

4. can play a musical instrument _____

5. likes playing volleyball _____

6. saw a movie last weekend _____

7. would like to be a teacher someday _____

8. knows who the principal (headmaster, director) of this school is _____

9. is going to college someday _____

10. was born in the same month as you _____

B Write a paragraph about yourself. Use some of the same kinds of information as in the questions you asked. For example, tell when and where you were born, how many brothers and sisters you have, how large a family you want, and so on.

_____

_____

_____

_____

_____

_____

_____

_____

_____

SKILL OBJECTIVES: Interviewing; giving an oral report; asking questions; writing a paragraph. Ask if anyone had a birthday recently or will have one soon. When is/was it? As responses are given, write them on the board: *Kim's birthday was yesterday, September 15; Juan's birthday is next week, September 20,* etc. Then have students practice asking when classmates' birthdays are. Ask other questions for oral practice, then tell students they are going to ask classmates the questions on the page and try to get at least one "yes" answer to each question. Have them record their answers and report to the class. *Part B:* Assign this for independent written work.

Alternative Word Meanings

The dictionary often lists several meanings for one word.
Read the following dictionary entries. Decide which meaning
of the word is being used in each sentence. Write the number
of that definition in front of the sentence. The first one is done for you.

run
1. to move rapidly
2. to operate, work, or move
3. to manage; be in charge of
4. to take part in a race or election

   3   My father <u>runs</u> the supermarket on 12th Street.

_____ Paul Lopez is going to <u>run</u> for class president.

_____ There's my bus. I've got to <u>run</u>!

_____ My car <u>runs</u> best on premium gas.

note
1. reputation or fame
2. a musical sound
3. a short letter

_____ The song ended on a sweet <u>note</u>.

_____ Jason's mother wrote his teacher a <u>note</u>.

_____ Henry Larkin is a musician of some <u>note</u>.

fly
1. to move through the air with wings
2. to pass quickly
3. to wave in the air
4. to travel by aircraft

_____ Paul Peterson, the reporter, has to <u>fly</u> to the West Coast often.

_____ Most birds <u>fly</u> south for the winter.

_____ Time does <u>fly</u> when you're having fun.

_____ <u>Fly</u> the flag proudly, boys.

poor
1. needy; having too little money
2. unhappy; deserving pity
3. unsatisfactory; not good

_____ Your <u>poor</u> performance on this test shows that you didn't study.

_____ There are many <u>poor</u> people in this city.

_____ Look at that <u>poor</u>, wet cat.

carry
1. to have for sale
2. to win
3. to hold up; support
4. to pick up and bring

_____ José, can you <u>carry</u> these books downstairs, please?

_____ This little wagon can <u>carry</u> over 100 pounds.

_____ Did the Democrats <u>carry</u> this state in the last election?

_____ This store doesn't <u>carry</u> calendars.

SKILL OBJECTIVES: Choosing the correct definition; building vocabulary. Review the directions, then do the first set of sentences as a group activity. Assign the page as independent work. *Extension Activity:* Students can write sentences illustrating two or three different meanings of some of these words: *light, fair, block, hand, match, fall, figure, head.* They may use their dictionaries for help.

5

200 Years of American History

Answer the following questions in complete sentences, using the time line to help you. Remember to write all your answers In the past tense. The first one is done for you.

1775 ┤1775 Revolutionary War begins
    ├1776 Declaration of Independence
    ├1787 Constitution written
    ├1789 Washington becomes first president
1800 ┤
    ├1803 Jefferson purchases Louisiana from France
1825 ┤
    ├1836 Texas becomes independent republic
    ├1845 Texas joins the U.S.
    ├1846 Mexican-American War begins
1850 ┤

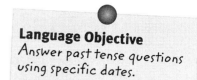

    ├1861 Civil War begins
    ├1865 Civil War ends
    ├1867 U.S. purchases Alaska
    ├1869 Railroads link east coast and west coast
1875 ┤

    ├1898 Spanish-American War
1900 ┤
    ├1917 U.S. enters World War I
    ├1920 Women allowed to vote nationwide
1925 ┤
    ├1929 Great Depression begins
    ├1941 Pearl Harbor. U.S. enters World War II
    ├1945 World War II ends
1950 ┤1950 Korean War begins
    ├1959 Alaska and Hawaii become states
    ├1961 U.S. enters Vietnam War
    ├1969 U.S. puts first man on the moon
1975 ┤1975 Vietnam War ends

1. When did the United States enter the Vietnam War?

   The United States entered the Vietnam War in 1961.

2. When did Texas join the United States?

   _____

3. When did Thomas Jefferson purchase Louisiana from France?

   _____

4. When did Alaska and Hawaii become states?

   _____

5. When did women get the right to vote nationwide?

   _____

6. When did the Civil War begin?

   _____

7. When did the Great Depression begin?

   _____

8. When did Washington become president?

   _____

9. When did World War II end?

   _____

10. When did railroads link the east and west?

   _____

SKILL OBJECTIVES: Interpreting a time line; sequencing. Have volunteers read the notations on the time line aloud. Help with reading dates and with vocabulary, if necessary. Then go through the ten questions orally, having students answer in complete sentences. If students have additional knowledge about any of the events or places, encourage discussion. Have students complete the page independently. Remind them to write their answers in complete sentences.

Affirmative and Negative

A The time line on the facing page will show you that the following statements are *false*. Change these statements to *true* by changing the affirmative to the negative. The first one is done for you.

1. The Civil War began in 1864.   *The Civil War didn't begin in 1864.*

2. Women were able to vote nationwide before 1920. _____

_____

3. Texas became a republic in 1845. _____

_____

4. The Civil War lasted ten years. _____

_____

5. Korea puts the first man on the moon. _____

_____

6. The Korean War came before World War II. _____

_____

7. Thomas Jefferson was the first president of the United States. _____

_____

B The following statements are answers to questions. Write the question under each answer. The first one is done for you.

1. George Washington became president in 1789.

   When   *did George Washington become president?*

2. The Revolutionary War lasted for eight years.

   How long _____?

3. Alaska and Hawaii became states in 1959.

   When _____?

4. The United States entered World War II because the Japanese bombed Pearl Harbor.

   Why _____?

5. The Civil War began at Fort Sumter in South Carolina.

   Where _____?

6. Jefferson purchased the Louisiana Territory in 1803.

   What _____?

7. Texas was an independent republic from 1836 to 1845.

   How long _____?

SKILL OBJECTIVES: Forming negative sentences; asking questions. Write on the board, *Alaska and Hawaii became states in 1969.* Ask if the sentence is true. Have students check the time line on the previous page for the answer (it's not true). Have students form the negative past: *Alaska and Hawaii didn't become …* Write, *When …?* Have students form the correct past question form, *When did …?* answering orally. After a few more examples on the board, assign the page for independent written work. As an option, you may wish to go through the whole page orally before assigning it for written work.

7

Getting to Know You

Language Objectives
Define vocabulary. Answer questions about a reading. Outline a reading.

A Make sure you know the meaning of these words which are underlined in the article.

personalities	ended	mules	talented	architecture
famous	tobacco	continued	foreign	designed

B Read the article quickly to get some general ideas about it. Then read it again more slowly to answer the questions.

Presidents with Personality

George Washington, John Adams, and Thomas Jefferson were the first three presidents of the United States. You may have already learned about some of their many accomplishments. But what do you know about the personalities of these famous men?

George Washington was a serious and disciplined person. But he also liked to have fun. He gave many parties. But all his party guests were sent home by 9 o'clock so he could get to bed early. When his second term ended, President Washington retired to his home in Virginia. It is called Mount Vernon. Washington liked fishing and hunting. He also liked farming. He grew tobacco and raised mules at Mount Vernon.

John Adams grew up on a farm in Massachusetts. He was intelligent and liked studying law and history. John Adams was George Washington's vice president. He didn't like this job much. He thought it was "insignificant." John Adams was elected the next president and he preferred this position. His vice president was Thomas Jefferson. The two men were friends but had different political views. Adams and Jefferson were at odds with each other. When Jefferson was elected the next president,

Adams was angry. Before Jefferson was sworn in, Adams left without speaking to him. He returned to his home in Massachusetts. There, he continued what he liked to do. He studied and wrote about politics. Eventually, he made peace with Thomas Jefferson. John Adams wrote many famous letters to the next president.

Thomas Jefferson was a very talented man. Like the first two presidents, he lived on a farm. He liked riding horses and hunting. Thomas Jefferson had many other interests. He played the violin and sang. He studied several foreign languages. He spoke Latin, Greek, Italian, French, and Spanish. After Jefferson was president, he returned to his home in Virginia, which was called Monticello. He returned also to one of his other interests, architecture. He designed several buildings for the University of Virginia.

These three presidents were real people. They had likes and dislikes. They had interests in many things other than their jobs. Finding out about their personalities is part of the fun of learning. Go to the library or online and discover the real people who made history!

C Think carefully and answer the following question.

According to the article, what was George Washington most probably doing by 10 o'clock at night?

a. having a party

c. writing letters

b. sleeping

d. planting tobacco

(Go on to the next page.)

SKILL OBJECTIVES: Reading comprehension; building vocabulary. Review the directions with the students. After the first reading, you may wish to lead a discussion about the meaning of the highlighted vocabulary words. Encourage students to check and refine their definitions by using a dictionary.

D What is the main idea of the article? Circle the best answer.

a. Washington, Adams, and Jefferson were famous.

b. Washington, Adams, and Jefferson were presidents with interesting personalities.

c. Washington, Adams, and Jefferson lived on farms.

d. Washington, Adams, and Jefferson were friends.

E Use a word from the underlined vocabulary list to complete each sentence.

1. Alice can sing, dance, and play the piano. She is very _____.

2. James Bond is a _____ character in books and movies.

3. The painting class began at 9 o'clock and _____ at 12 o'clock.

4. For a person who speaks only Spanish, English is a _____ language.

5. Who _____ this beautiful building?

F Answer these questions in your notebook.

1. Who were the first three presidents of the United States?

2. Why did George Washington's parties end by 9 o'clock?

3. What was the name of George Washington's home?

4. In which state did John Adams live?

5. What job did John Adams dislike?

6. Who did John Adams write letters to?

7. In which state did Thomas Jefferson live?

8. What foreign languages did Thomas Jefferson learn?

9. What did Thomas Jefferson design?

G Complete this outline of the article by listing things the presidents liked to do.

1. George Washington liked to:

a. _____

b. _____

c. _____

2. John Adams liked to:

a. _____

b. _____

c. _____

3. Thomas Jefferson liked to:

a. _____

b. _____

c. _____

SKILL OBJECTIVES: Identifying main ideas and details; building vocabulary; outlining. Students should complete these exercises independently. Correct and discuss the page as a class. *Extension Activity*: Interested students can use the encyclopedia to find out facts about the childhoods of these three presidents. They should write down these facts in outline form. Remind students to skim each article, using the headings, to find the section that deals specifically with that president's early life.

A Busy Morning

A Look at the picture story of Jane's morning. Use it to fill in the blanks in the paragraph below. The first one is done for you.

Jane got up late yesterday morning. She ran _____*into*_____ the bathroom, brushed her _____, and washed her face. Then she _____ into the kitchen and looked in _____ refrigerator. She decided to have only _____ because she was late. While she _____ drinking her coffee, she quickly _____ the morning newspaper. After breakfast, she _____ dressed, left her apartment, _____ ran to the bus stop. Unfortunately, _____ missed the bus and had to _____ for the next one.

B Now read each of the statements below and look at the picture story. Write *T* if the statement is true. Write *F* if the statement is false. Write *?* if the story does not give you enough information to decide if the statement is true or false. The first one is done for you.

1. Jane got up at 8:00 yesterday.   ___?___

2. She brushed her teeth before breakfast.   _____

3. She had a large breakfast.   _____

4. She got dressed before breakfast.   _____

5. She hurried to the bus stop.   _____

6. She waited fifteen minutes for the bus.   _____

SKILL OBJECTIVES: Using pictures to complete a story; distinguishing between *true, false,* and *?*. Have students look at the picture story and tell you what Jane did yesterday. *Part A:* Explain that one word is missing from each blank and students are to fill in that word. There may be more than one correct answer for any blank: *to* would be as correct as *into* for the first one. Explain that students must follow the pictures to fill in the blanks. If necessary, go through the exercise orally before assigning it for independent written work. *Part B:* Be sure students understand when to use the *?*: Jane may or may not have gotten up at 8:00, but the story doesn't tell us.

Word Skills: Homophones

Some words in English sound exactly alike but have different spellings and meanings. These words are called *homophones*. Here are some examples of homophones.

He <u>ate eight</u> eggs.

She <u>rode</u> down the <u>road</u>.

My <u>son</u> is playing in the <u>sun</u>.

Complete the following sentences. Use the words in the Data Bank. Your dictionary will help you choose the correct homophone. The first one is done for you.

1. He is a vegetarian; he doesn't eat _____ *meat.* _____

2. Mei Lee knows how to _____ her own clothes.

3. There are sixty minutes in one _____

4. Yesterday, there was a big _____ at the department store.

5. The Sampsons are going to visit _____ daughter.

6. Sonia traveled to California by _____.

7. Raoul is shopping; he wants a new _____ of shoes.

8. Everyone wants to go _____ the movies tonight.

9. Speak a little louder, please. I can't _____ you.

10. Please _____ here until the boys come out.

11. The Turners are going to _____ a new car.

12. Walk to the end of the street and turn _____.

13. The girls _____ the answer, but I don't.

14. Rita received three letters in today's _____.

15. The students stayed in New York last _____.

16. Sally got a piece of sand in her _____ at the beach yesterday.

DATA BANK			
by / buy / bye	~~meat / meet~~	plane / plain	their / there / they're
eye / I	no / know	right / write	to / two / too
here / hear	our / hour	sail / sale	wait / weight
mail / male	pear / pair / pare	so / sew	weak / week

SKILL OBJECTIVE: Distinguishing between homophones. Review the definition of homophones and go over the three illustrated examples with the class. Complete several items as a group, then assign the page as independent written work. *Extension Activity:* Encourage students to use the homophones in the Data Bank to write sentences similar to the three at the top of this page. Each sentence should contain two or more homophones. Example: *I feel weak this week.*

Dear Dot

Dear Dot,

Last week I was playing tennis with my boyfriend, Jimmy. We played three matches, and I was the winner every time. Jimmy was very angry. He said he was never going to play tennis with me again. I like tennis because it is such good exercise. How can I convince Jimmy to continue playing tennis with me?

Chrissy

1. When were Chrissy and Jimmy playing tennis? _____

_____

2. How many matches did they play? _____

3. Why do you think Jimmy was angry? _____

_____

4. What did Jimmy say to Chrissy? _____

_____

5. Why does Chrissy like to play tennis? _____

_____

6. What does the word *convince* mean as used in this letter? Circle the best answer.

   a. beat   **b.** bother   **c.** bring   **d.** talk into

7. What is your advice to Chrissy? Discuss your answer in class. Then read Dot's answer, and tell why you agree or disagree. Dot's advice is below.

Dear Chrissy,
   Try talking to Jimmy. Does he really want you not to play just as well as you can? Does he really think that men have to be superior to women? If he does (or you think that he does), find another tennis partner. And think about Jimmy's attitude before you get too serious with him.
Dot

SKILL OBJECTIVES: Reading comprehension; understanding words through context; making judgments. Have students read the letter and answer the questions independently. If you wish, have students write their advice to Chrissy in their notebooks. Correct the page as a class, then have students compare and discuss their own advice and Dot's reply. You may want to raise these questions for discussion: *Why do you think Jimmy got angry? How do you think Jimmy would have acted if he had lost the match to another boy?*

12

Sam tries to be sensible about eating. This chart shows some of the things he does. Look at the chart, then follow the instructions below it.

	Always	Usually	Sometimes	Seldom	Never
1. Eats a good breakfast	X				
2. Has a bowl of cereal with fruit		X			
3. Has two scrambled eggs			X		
4. Drinks cola for breakfast					X
5. Brings lunch to school			X		
6. Buys lunch in cafeteria			X		
7. Skips lunch				X	
8. Eats dinner with his family at 6:30	X				
9. Helps in the kitchen after dinner		X			

A Use the chart to write about Sam. The first two sentences are done for you.

Sam tries to eat sensibly. He always eats a good breakfast.

_____

_____

_____

_____

_____

_____

B Now write about you. Use *always, usually, sometimes, seldom, never*.

_____

_____

_____

_____

_____

_____

SKILL OBJECTIVES: Adverbs of frequency; interpreting a chart. Read the introductory lines aloud, then ask questions about the chart. *What does Sam (always, hardly ever, etc.) do? Does Sam (always) bring lunch to school?* Encourage students to ask each other similar questions. Assign the page for independent written work. *Extension Activity*: Have students write about their daily schedules, using each adverb of frequency at least once. These questions may help focus their thoughts: *When do you get up? What do you do before/after school? What do you do at night?*

Counting Calories

A calorie is a measure of the energy you get from food. If the food you eat supplies more calories than you use up, you gain weight. If it supplies fewer calories than you use up, you lose weight. The menu below shows how many calories are in some foods many Americans eat for breakfast, lunch, and dinner.

MENU

Breakfast	Calories	Lunch	Calories	Dinner	Calories
orange juice (1 cup)	110	hamburger (4 oz.)	320	fried chicken (6 oz.)	520
1 fried egg	95	bread roll	120	broiled chicken (6 oz.)	320
1 boiled egg	80	1 can of cola (12 oz.)	150	1 boiled potato	125
whole wheat toast	55	French fries (1 cup)	570	1 cup peas	120
1 pat butter	50	1 banana	95	1 slice French bread	120
2 slices bacon	90	tomato juice (1/2 cup)	25	1 cup squash	100
coffee		tuna salad (1/2 cup)	180	3 pats butter	150
1 tsp. whole milk	20	1 slice Syrian bread	80	1 cup whole milk	175
1 tsp. sugar	18	1 medium apple	75	1 cup skim milk	75
cup coffee/skim milk	0	1 can of diet cola (12 oz.)	1	1 cup gelatin dessert	140

A Use the menu to complete these sentences.

1. One slice of bacon has _____ calories.

2. Syrian bread has (more / fewer) calories than whole wheat bread. (Circle one.)

3. There are _____ more calories in a cup of whole milk than in a cup of skim milk.

4. Six ounces of broiled chicken has _____ fewer calories than six ounces of fried chicken.

5. There are _____ calories in one cup of tomato juice.

6. An apple has _____ fewer calories than a banana.

7. A hamburger, including the roll, has _____ calories.

8. A can of regular cola has _____ more calories than a can of diet cola.

9. A fried egg has _____ more calories than a boiled egg.

10. Two bananas have _____ calories.

11. A breakfast of a boiled egg, one slice of whole wheat toast, 1/2 pat of butter, and 1/2 cup of orange juice has _____ calories.

12. A breakfast of a fried egg, one slice of bacon, one slice of whole wheat toast, and a cup of black coffee has _____ calories.

13. A tuna salad (1/2 cup) sandwich on whole wheat bread has _____ calories.

B Susan's doctor says she must go on a diet of 1,400 calories a day. In your notebook, write a nutritious breakfast, lunch, and dinner for Susan with no more than 1,400 calories. Use foods from the menu above.

SKILL OBJECTIVES: Using charts to solve word problems; devising a diet. Read the sentences at the top of the page with the class and give students time to look at the menu. Answer any questions about it. *Part A:* Do several items orally with the class, and be sure students understand how to use the menu to answer the questions. Assign for independent work. *Part B:* Call on volunteers to plan a sample nutritious breakfast for Susan. Then have students do plans for lunch and dinner. Remind them that all three meals must add up to no more than 1,400 calories. The meals should include meats (or fish, dairy), fruits and vegetables, and bread.

In the Kitchen (1)

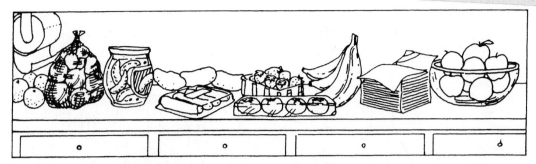

Look at the picture of the kitchen counter. Use it to answer the questions. Where the answers are given, make up questions to go with them. The first three are done for you.

1. Are there any apples in this kitchen?   _Yes, there are many._____

2. Are there any pears in this kitchen?   _No, there aren't any. (or "are none")_

3. Are there any oranges in this kitchen?   _Yes, there are some. (or "a few")___

4. Are there any cookies in this kitchen?   _____

5. Are there any napkins?   _____

6. Are there any bananas?   _____

7. Are there any eggs?   _____

8. Are there any lemons?   _____

9. Are there any sandwiches for lunch?   _____

10. Are there any pickles?   _____

11. Are there any tomatoes?   _____

12. Are there any lamb chops?   _____

13. Are there any paper towels?   _____

14. _____?   Yes, there are a few.

15. _____?   No, there aren't any.

16. _____?   Yes, there are many.

17. _____?   No, there are none.

18. How many hot dog rolls are there?   _____

19. How many hot dogs are there?   _____

20. How many potatoes are there?   _____

In the Kitchen (2)

Mr. Garcia has come back from the supermarket and is putting away the things he bought. Look at the picture and answer the questions about Mr. Garcia's groceries. Where the answers are given, make up questions to go with them. The first three are done for you.

1. Is there any corn? _Yes, there is a lot._

2. Is there any tuna fish? _No, there isn't any. (or "is none")_

3. Is there any lettuce? _Yes, there is some. (or "a little")_

4. Is there any orange juice? _____

5. Is there any sugar? _____

6. Is there any soap? _____

7. Is there any bread? _____

8. Is there any bacon? _____

9. Is there any ketchup? _____

10. Is there any salad oil? _____

11. Is there any cereal? _____

12. Is there any toothpaste? _____

13. Is there any cake? _____

14. _____? Yes, there is some.

15. _____? No, there isn't any.

16. How much soup is there? _____

17. How much rice is there? _____

18. How much butter is there? _____

SKILL OBJECTIVE: Asking/answering quantity questions with non-count nouns. Write: *Is there any ...? How much ... is there?* Teach the adverbs of quantity: *a lot, quite a lot, some, a little, none/any.* Have students ask/answer questions about the picture. Draw a 1/4 –filled ketchup bottle, a stack of soap, two eggs, and ten oranges. Ask, *How much ketchup/soap is there? How many eggs/oranges are there? (a little, a lot; a few, many)* Note the different adverbs used with count *vs.* non-count nouns.

Sam's Place

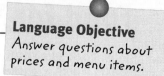

OPEN 7 DAYS   6 a.m–11 p.m. MON.–FRI.   9 a.m.–11 p.m. SAT. & SUN.

—SUBS—

	SM.	LG.		SM.	LG.		SM.	LG.
Cold Cuts	4.95	5.95	Corned Beef	5.95	6.95	Smoked Turkey	4.95	5.95
Roast Beef	5.95	6.95	Genoa Salami	4.95	5.95	Smoked Ham	4.95	5.95
Pastrami	5.95	6.95	Honey Turkey	4.95	5.95	Virginia Ham	5.95	6.95

—Try the hot ones—

	SM.	LG.		SM.	LG.		SM.	LG.
Grilled Chicken	4.00	5.00	Steak	5.00	6.00	Tuna Melt	4.75	5.75
Chicken Cutlet	4.00	5.00	Steak & Peppers	5.75	6.75	Meatball	4.00	5.00
Fresh Turkey	4.75	5.75	Sausage & Peppers	4.00	5.00	Meatball Parmiagiana	4.75	5.75

—PIZZA WITH PIZZAZZ— *Buy 3 Pizzas—Get One Free*

	SM.	LG.		SM.	LG.		SM.	LG.
Cheese	6.00	8.00	Sausage	6.95	8.95	Tomato/Basil	6.95	8.95
Onion	6.50	8.50	Pepperoni	6.95	8.95	Olive	6.50	8.50
Pepper	6.50	8.50	Mushroom	7.00	9.00	Any 2 Combo	7.25	10.00

Pizza Served Mon.–Thurs. 5–11 p.m. Fri.–Sun. 4–11 p.m.

BEVERAGES

Soda	1.50	Coffee	1.50
Milk	.75	Tea	1.50
Juice	2.00		

SIDE SPECIALS

French Fries LG: 3.00
SM: 1.75

Salads
Tuna   7.95
Greek 7.00
Garden 6.95

Look at Sam's menu. Use your dictionary for words you do not know. (You may not find *sub*. It is a kind of sandwich made with a loaf of French bread that is split from end to end, and it has different names in different parts of the country.) Now answer the questions about Sam's menu. Use short answers.

1. Why are there two prices for each sub? _____

2. How much is a corned beef sub? _____

3. What kinds of salads does Sam's offer? _____

4. How much is a small cold cut sub with a small order of French fries? _____

5. "Combo" stands for combination. What do you think a combo pizza is? _____
   _____

6. How much is a small pizza with cheese and sausage? _____

7. Maria bought four pizzas. How many did she have to pay for? _____

8. Can you buy a pizza for lunch at Sam's? _____

9. Is a large pepperoni pizza the same price as a large mushroom pizza? _____

10. How much is a Greek salad and a can of orange juice? _____

11. Is Sam's open every day? _____

12. You are buying lunch for yourself and four friends. How much is a small honey turkey sub, a large tuna melt sub, a Greek salad, a small pastrami sub, a garden salad, and five sodas? _____

13. How much will you pay for three small tuna melts and two large coffees? _____

14. Do they probably sell ginger ale at Sam's Place? _____

SKILL OBJECTIVES: Interpreting a menu; solving mathematical word problems. Explain any unfamiliar words on the menu. Ask various students, *What would you like for lunch?* ("I'd like …") Prompt with additional questions, *Is that a large or a small (sub)? What would you like to drink?* Write the order on the board. Have the class compute the bill. Assign the page for independent written work. *Extension Activity:* Have students role play ordering lunch at Sam's Place, paying their bill, and leaving a tip.

Food for Your Health

A Make sure you know the meaning of the following important words which are underlined in the article.

necessary	major	poultry	prevent
health	specific	digest	bleeding

B Read the article quickly to get some general ideas about it. Then read it again more slowly to answer the questions.

Vitamins

Vitamins are <u>necessary</u> for good <u>health</u>. We get vitamins from the foods that we eat. There are about ten <u>major</u> vitamins. Each vitamin has a <u>specific</u> job to do in the body. Read about vitamins below.

- **Vitamin A**—Vitamin A comes from green and yellow vegetables. It is also in milk and egg yolks. Vitamin A is necessary for night vision (seeing in the dark).

- **Vitamin B_1**—Vitamin B_1 comes from fish, brown rice, and <u>poultry</u>. It is also in most meats and nuts. The job of vitamin B_1 is to build the blood and help the body <u>digest</u> food.

- **Vitamin B_{12}**—Vitamin B_{12} comes from cheese, fish, and milk. The job of vitamin B_{12} is to build up the red blood cells and to keep the body's nervous system healthy.

- **Vitamin C**—Vitamin C comes from citrus fruits such as oranges and grapefruit and other fruits such as strawberries. It is also in green peppers. Vitamin C is important in building bones and teeth, and some people say it helps to <u>prevent</u> colds.

- **Vitamin D**—Vitamin D comes from egg yolks. In the United States, the dairy industry also adds it to milk. People also get vitamin D from sunlight. Vitamin D is important for building strong bones.

- **Vitamin E**—Vitamin E comes from dark green vegetables such as spinach. It is also found in eggs and liver. Vitamin E is important in reproduction and muscle development.

- **Vitamin K**—Vitamin K comes from green leafy vegetables and yogurt. Its job is to help the blood to clot. Without vitamin K, cuts and scrapes keep <u>bleeding</u>. Vitamin K helps the cut to close. It keeps the body from losing too much blood.

C Think carefully and answer the following question.

According to the article, which of the following is most likely to contain Vitamin A?

a. rice   **b.** liver   **c.** oranges   **d.** broccoli

(Go on to the next page.)

SKILL OBJECTIVES: Reading comprehension; drawing conclusions; building vocabulary. Review the directions with the students. After the first reading, you may wish to lead a discussion about the meaning of the highlighted vocabulary. Encourage students to check and refine their understanding of the words by using a dictionary.

D **Circle the answer that best completes the sentence.**

Vitamins are necessary for good health because

    a. they are found in certain foods.

    b. they have important jobs to do in the body.

    c. there are ten major vitamins.

    d. they are chemical substances.

E **Use a word from the underlined vocabulary to complete each of these sentences.**

    1. Quick, get a bandage! Diana's foot is _____.

    2. Smoking is the _____ cause of lung cancer.

    3. I don't understand your problem; please be more _____.

    4. Don't let accidents happen; try to _____ them.

    5. Most people agree that a balanced diet and exercise are the key to good _____.

F **Answer these questions in your notebook. (Number your answers to match the questions.)**

    1. What are three vitamins that come from green vegetables?

    2. What vitamin does brown rice contain?

    3. What vitamin do both egg yolks and sunlight provide?

    4. What vitamin helps keep the nervous system healthy?

    5. What vitamin helps blood to clot?

    6. What does "clot" mean?

    7. What fruits give us a good supply of vitamin C?

    8. What foods give us a good supply of vitamin E?

    9. What vitamin helps the body to digest food?

  10. What is night vision?

G **Look at the list of foods below. They have lots of vitamins. Are they part of your diet (what you eat)? Complete the chart by checking if you eat lots, some, or none of each of the foods on the list.**

	Lots of	Some	None
liver			
milk			
eggs			
fish			
nuts			
poultry			
green vegetables			
fruits			
rice			

SKILL OBJECTIVES: Identifying main idea and details; building vocabulary; charting information. Students should complete these exercises independently. Correct and discuss as a class. *Extension Activity:* Have groups research the following questions in an encyclopedia, first deciding under which entries they will look: *Why is it important to get vitamin C every day? Which foods contain lots of iron, an essential mineral? What happens to people who don't get enough iron? What vitamins are found in carrots? In tomatoes?*

Beginnings and Endings

Language Objective
Combine clauses using context clues to make complex sentences.

Find the right ending for each sentence, and write its letter in the blank. Each letter may be used only once. The first one is done for you.

1. Lisa always studies, so ___j___
2. Pablo always gets up late, so _____
3. Chang never eats breakfast, so _____
4. Mr. Watson seldom drives his car, so _____
5. The baby usually sleeps in the afternoon, so _____
6. Luis is always smiling, so _____
7. Peter frequently drives fast, so _____
8. Dulce doesn't know what's happening in the world because _____
9. My little sister sometimes gets sick because _____
10. Wanda's boss is very angry at her because _____
11. Jill doesn't buy much at the cafeteria because _____
12. All the students want Mei Ling on their team because _____
13. Mr. Fell's students study hard every Thursday night because _____
14. Because it usually rains on weekends, _____
15. Because that store closes at 5:00, _____
16. Because Michael almost never eats sugar, _____
17. Because my uncle seldom writes letters, _____
18. Because English often is confusing, _____
19. Because the students sometimes are noisy, _____
20. Because my father always plays chess at my uncle's house on Friday night, _____

a. he's very hungry at lunch.
b. she always hits a home run.
c. we stay inside on Saturday and Sunday.
d. we have to be quiet when we get home from school.
e. the teacher has to tell them to be quiet.
f. he gets a lot of tickets.
g. his teeth are in good condition.
h. she eats too much.
i. you have to shop early.
j. she gets good grades on her report card.
k. we call him on the phone every month.
l. she usually brings her lunch.
m. people are glad to see him.
n. he comes home late.
o. he often misses his first class.
p. you have to study it very carefully.
q. she almost never watches the news on TV.
r. he gives tests on Friday.
s. it is in good condition.
t. she often misses work.

SKILL OBJECTIVES: **Noting cause and effect; using *so*, *because*.** Write on the board: *Lisa always studies, so she gets good grades. Lisa gets good grades because she always studies. Because she always studies, Lisa gets good grades.* Let students agree that all three sentences mean the same. Assign the page as written work. *Extension Activity:* Have students complete these sentences: *Angela didn't feel well, so ... Because I missed the last bus home ... My father doesn't like winter because ...*

Word Skills: Antonyms

Language Objective
Use context clues to answer questions with pairs of opposites.

Antonyms are words that are opposite in meaning. *High* and *low* are antonyms because *high* is the opposite of *low*. Not every word has an antonym, but many do. Here are some common English antonyms. Read the list and then answer the questions under it.

always / never	clean / dirty	right / left	before / after
often / seldom	open / close	in / out	big / little
question / answer	dead / alive	start / finish	day / night
arrive / leave	east / west	stop / go	near / far
awake / asleep	first / last	on / off	hello / goodbye
begin / end	front / back	up / down	hot / cold
buy / sell	love / hate		

1. Which antonym pair describes what people do in a store? _____

2. Which antonym pair describes directions on a map? _____

3. Which antonym pair describes a race? _____

4. Which antonym pair describes a red light and a green light? _____

5. Which antonym pair describes strong emotions? _____

6. Which antonym pair describes the weather? _____

7. Which antonym pair describes an elephant and an ant? _____

8. Which antonym pair describes sunlight and moonlight? _____

9. Which antonym pair describes a school test? _____

10. Which antonym pair describes out of bed or in bed? _____

11. Which antonym pair describes distances? _____

12. Which antonym pair describes car turn signals? _____

13. Which antonym pair describes stairways? _____

14. Which antonym pair describes a fast conversation? _____

15. Which antonym pair describes an electrical appliance? _____

16. Which antonym pair describes what a train does? _____

17. Which antonym pair describes the two covers of a book? _____

18. Which antonym pair describes what you do to a door? _____

SKILL OBJECTIVES: Understanding antonyms; classifying. Say the following words, and have the class name the opposites: *yes, fat, early, young, win, empty, fast, wet, happy, summer, wonderful, tall, pretty.* Read the directions with the class and have students read the list of antonyms. Then assign the page as independent written work. Discuss the answers as a class.

Call the Doctor!

Most people are healthy most of the time, but now and then people do not feel well. Some people have serious illnesses or conditions, some have temporary sicknesses that are less serious, and some have diseases that they have "caught" from other people. Look at the three lists below. Use your dictionary or an encyclopedia to find out about each of the items on the lists.

Language Objectives
Match ailments and symptoms. Name the doctors who take care of specific problems.

Illness/Condition	Sickness	Communicable Diseases
diabetes	flu (virus)	chicken pox
heart trouble	fever	German measles
cancer	headache, earache,	measles
allergy	backache, etc.	mumps
asthma	stomachache	scarlet fever

A Look at the list of conditions at the left. Draw a line from each condition to the symptoms (the way you feel or the effects of the condition) at the right. The first one is done for you. Use your dictionary or an encyclopedia to help you.

1. headache
2. allergy
3. chicken pox
4. fever
5. stomachache
6. diabetes
7. heart trouble
8. flu

a. you have a temperature of 102°F
b. you feel like throwing up your food
c. your body can't use sugar and you need insulin shots
d. you have a headache, sore throat, fever, earache, and cold
e. your heart is weak
f. children get red spots on their bodies
g. you sneeze from dust, flowers, and animals
h. your head hurts

B Different kinds of doctors take care of different kinds of diseases or conditions. Use words from the Data Bank to complete each of these sentences. Use your dictionary if you need to.

1. When a woman is going to have a baby, she goes to a(n) _____ .
2. After the baby is born, she takes it to a(n) _____ .
3. A family doctor who treats common illnesses is a(n) _____ .
4. If you have a toothache, you go to a(n) _____ .
5. If you have to have your appendix removed, you go to a(n) _____ .
6. If you are having trouble with your eyes, you go to a(n) _____ .
7. People who are very depressed can go to a(n) _____ .

DATA BANK			
dentist	general practitioner	obstetrician	ophthalmologist
pediatrician	psychiatrist	surgeon	

C In your notebook, write the names of other kinds of doctors and tell what they do. Use an encyclopedia to find this information.

SKILL OBJECTIVES: Building vocabulary; discussing illnesses and symptoms. Read the introduction with the class. Have students study the charts, using a dictionary when needed. Discuss the symptoms of the different ailments and how each illness can be treated. Ask students which illnesses they have had. Assign Parts A and B for independent or pair work. Part C may be done as homework. A group list of the names and descriptions of medical specialists can then be compiled.

Follow the Directions

When you take any kind of medicine, it is important to follow the directions for that medicine. Your medicine may be either something prescribed by a doctor and supplied to you by a pharmacist in a drugstore or something that anyone can buy from a drugstore counter.

A When a doctor believes you need a special kind of medicine, he or she writes a prescription. You take the prescription to the pharmacist who gives you the medicine. The label on the container tells you what the medicine is and how often you should take it. Look at this label. Use it to answer the questions.

STONE PHARMACY R_X
Jason Stone, Reg. Pharm.
Tel. 555-0225

Rx No. 806-943   Date 7/2/04

Catherine Cook
14 Main St,
Yorktown, NY.

Take 1 one tablet every 4 hours, as directed by physician.

Pen VK
250 mg.

Dr. Eli Morton

1. Who is the medicine for? _____

2. Is Jason Stone the doctor or the pharmacist? _____

3. What is the number of the prescription? _____

4. Pen VK is penicillin. What is penicillin? _____

5. Is Pen VK a liquid? _____

6. How often does Catherine have to take her medicine? _____

7. What is the name of the drugstore? _____

B Most medicines that you buy from the drugstore counter have directions on the container. Look at this set of directions from an aspirin bottle and use it to answer the questions.

1. Why do people take aspirin? _____
_____

2. What is the recommended adult dosage?
_____

3. What is the recommended dosage for children aged 6 to 12? _____

4. What should parents of a child under 6 do before they give their child aspirin?
_____

5. Should you keep this bottle in the refrigerator? _____

Aspirin is used for relief of simple headache and for temporary relief of minor arthritic pain, the discomfort and fever of colds or "flu," menstrual cramps, muscular aches from fatigue, and toothache. Dosage: 2 tablets every four hours as needed. Do not exceed 12 tablets in 24 hours unless directed by physician. For children 6–12, one-half dose. Under 6, consult physician. **Warning: Keep this and all medicines out of children's each. In case of accidental overdose, consult physician immediately. Caution:** If pain persists for more than 10 days or redness is present or in arthritic or rheumatic conditions affecting children under 12, consult a physician immediately. Do not take without consulting a physician if under medical care. Consult a dentist for toothache promptly. **Active ingredient:** Aspirin, 5 gr.

STORE AT ROOM TEMPERATURE

SKILL OBJECTIVE: Reading medical prescriptions and labels. Read the introductory paragraphs together, then assign the page as independent written work. *Extension Activity:* As a homework assignment, have students go to a drugstore land write down Ohe names and uses of five nonprescription drugs or health products. Have students bring in their lists to share with the class. Students may wish to discuss ways of treating health problems other than using these products.

Dear Dot

Dear Dot,

My son, Ronald, never goes out. He comes home from school and changes his clothes, and then he practices the piano. He plays for hours. After dinner he does his homework, and then he goes right back to his music. He doesn't have any friends. He never watches TV, and he never goes to the movies. Is he all right? I worry about him.

Concerned Mother

1. What does Ronald do after he changes his clothes? _____

_____

2. What does Ronald do when he isn't playing the piano? _____

_____

3. Is Ronald a popular person? _____

4. What do you think Concerned Mother wants Ronald to do? _____

_____

5. What is the best meaning of *concerned*, as used in this letter? Circle your answer.

    a. late   **b.** worried   **c.** strong   **d.** angry

6. What is your advice to Concerned Mother? Discuss your answer in class. Then read Dot's answer and tell why you agree or disagree. Dot's advice is below.

Dear Mom,

It's easy to understand why you are concerned about Ronald. I agree that he doesn't behave the way most boys of his age do. However, if he wants to make his living as a musician, he needs to practice a lot. You can't and shouldn't try to force a social life on him. What you can do is encourage him, show your interest, and be ready to listen if he wants to share his thoughts. If you just want him to go out once in a while, why not get tickets to a concert and take him out as a special treat. But be sure it's his kind of music!

Dot

Write About It

In your notebook, write a paragraph describing your typical day. Tell what you do from the time you get up until you go to bed.

SKILL OBJECTIVES: Reading for details; drawing conclusions; understanding words through context; making judgments. Have students read the letter and answer the questions independently. Students can write their advice to "Concerned Mother" in their notebooks. Correct the first five questions as a class, then have students compare and discuss their own advice and Dot's reply. You may wish to assign the "Write About It" topic as homework.

Look at these advertisements for summer jobs. Use them to answer the questions.

YARD WORK
Mon, Wed, Fri afternoons. $8.00/hr. to start. Mowing, gardening, gen. maintenance. Call 332-0066 for appt.

MONTANO'S BAKERY
Baker's Assistant needed 6 days, 6 a.m.–12 noon. Apply 27 Chestnut St., Bixford. No phone calls, please.

BUS BOYS
Summer Only—at **Chef's Delight.** No experience necessary. Openings in Bixford and Yorktown. 5–10 p.m.

MOTHER'S HELPER NEEDED
For two small children, Mon–Fri, 9 a.m to 12 noon. Some light house-work. References required. Call for appointment 555-7531, between 2 and 5.

GAS STATION ATTENDANT
Gas & oil only. Prefer some experi-ence but will train right person. 10 a.m.–5 p.m. Good pay. Apply in person. MUTUAL OIL COMPANY, 194 Whiting St., Bixford.

CASHIER
Carl's Coffee Shop, 7 a.m.– 2 p.m., June 25 to Sept. 1 only. No experi-ence necessary. Apply in person, 33 Main St., Rockland.

1. For summer employment, many managers ask that you apply in person. Which jobs here request that you apply in person? _____

_____

2. Only one of the job listings tells you the salary. Which one is it? _____

3. Which job listings say they will take a person with no experience? _____

_____

4. Name two jobs that are mornings only. _____

5. Name one summer job that is evenings only. _____

6. Some summer jobs are part-time (about twenty hours a week). How many of these jobs are part-time? What are they? _____

7. Does the gas station attendant have to fix cars? _____

8. Will the mother's helper probably have to wash some dishes and vacuum some rugs?

Answer *Yes* or *No*. _____

DATA BANK			
experience	apply	train	employment
employer	part-time	salary	

Work Places

Read the following paragraphs. Tell where the people work.
The first one is done for you.

1. Bill comes to work every day at 7:00. He feeds the animals their breakfast. He makes sure they are feeling well. Right now, he is teaching a monkey to do a new trick.
Bill works ___in a zoo.___

2. Susan arrives at work at 8:00. She talks to the news director and the weather forecaster. At 12:00, her program begins. Right now, Susan is reading the news.
Susan works _____

3. Carlos reports to work at 8:30. He looks at some loan applications. People ask him about loans and different kinds of accounts every day. Right now, Carlos is helping a customer to open a new savings account.
Carlos works _____

4. Nancy Yu gets to work at 7:15. Every day she erases the front chalkboard and writes a new problem for the students to solve. Right now, she is making out a test for her third period class.
Nancy works _____

5. Dana and Pat work from 9:00 to 5:00. They work together. Every day they answer phones, file papers, and take orders from clients. Right now, they are both typing emails to suppliers.
Dana and Pat work _____

6. Dave begins work at 11:00 p.m. He works until 7:00 in the morning. Every night he stamps prices on cereal, pet food, canned goods, and soda. He arranges food neatly on the shelves. Right now, he is sweeping the floor. Dave wants everything to look good when the boss comes in.
Dave works _____

7. Alana gets to work at 6:00 a.m. Every day she sits in a tall glass building and watches airplanes take off and land. She talks to the pilots by radio. She tells them when it is their turn to take off. Right now, she is taking a break. Her job is very stressful.
Alana works _____

8. Lisa works part-time after school. She gets a list from the manager every afternoon. It tells her the rooms she has to clean. Lisa makes the beds and vacuums the rugs. Right now, she is polishing the woodwork in Room 106.
Lisa works _____

9. Lorraine works from 3:00 p.m. to 11:00 p.m. Every afternoon she checks on her patients. She gives them their medicine and takes their temperature. At night she reads their charts and prepares their medication for the morning. Right now, she is talking with a patient. She is helping him to relax.
Lorraine works _____

DATA BANK

airport   bank   hospital   hotel   office   school   supermarket   TV station   ~~zoo~~

SKILL OBJECTIVES: Drawing conclusions; building vocabulary. Assign this page for independent written work. *Extension Activity:* Give each student the name of a work place. The students will write short paragraphs, describing a worker's job at that place. The work place should not be mentioned by name. Students will then read the paragraphs aloud, and their classmates will guess the work place. *(Factory, restaurant, movie theater, art museum, pet shop, drugstore, insurance company, sporting goods store, clothing store, hairdresser, farm, construction site.)*

Application Forms

Language Objective
Practice filling out a job application form.

If you apply for a part-time job, you will probably be given an application form to fill out. Each company has its own kind of form. But the information you have to give the company is very much the same for all companies. You almost always have to give your name, address, telephone number, and Social Security number. You also have to give the names of the schools you have attended. In addition, companies want to know what other jobs you have had. Finally, they want the names of people who know you and are willing to tell about you. (Before you list such a person as a "reference," be sure to ask his or her permission.)

The sample form below gives you a place to write down this kind of information. Fill it out for yourself. You may want to make a copy to take with you when you apply for a job and have to fill out an application form.

PERSONAL DATA

Name _____ Social Security Number _____

Address _____

How long at this address _____

Telephone _____

EDUCATION

	Name and Location	Dates Attended (from–to)	Courses
Elementary School			
Junior High or Middle School			
High School			

PREVIOUS JOBS (list latest job first)

From–To	Name and Location of Employer	Supervisor	Position Held and Salary	Reason for Leaving

REFERENCES

		Name and Address	Telephone Number
Personal:	1.		
	2.		
	3.		
Business:	1.		
	2.		
	3.		

SKILL OBJECTIVE: Filling out an application form. Review this application form with the students, explaining any unfamiliar terms. Discuss possible appropriate responses to *Reason for Leaving* and *Business References*. Assign the page for independent written work. Provide individual help as needed.

Your Social Security

Read the article.

Social Security is a U.S. government program. It is a program to help workers when they retire or become disabled. It also helps a worker's family when a worker dies. To receive benefits, a worker needs to have a Social Security number, a job, and must make FICA (Federal Insurance Contributions Act) payments. This payment is a payroll tax based on the worker's salary. Employers pay half of this FICA payment and the worker pays the other half. If a worker is self-employed, he or she must make the full payment.

All workers in the United States must have a Social Security number. You do not have to be a U.S. citizen or even a permanent resident to have a Social Security number. But you cannot get a job without one.

If you need to apply for a Social Security number, go to the nearest Social Security office and fill out the application. You can also download application forms from the Social Security website: www.socialsecurity.gov. You will need to show at least two documents to prove your age, identity, U.S.citizenship, or lawful alien status. The documents you present must be original and must be verified before a Social Security number is given to you.

- People born in the United States: Present a birth certificate and at least one other recent form of photo ID.
- U.S. citizens born outside the United States: Present a U.S. consular report of birth, U.S. passport, Certificate of Citizenship, or Certificate of Naturalization, and at least one other recent form of photo ID.
- Alien status: Present an unexpired document issued by the Department of Homeland Security (DHS): Form I-551, I-94, I-688B or I-766, and at least one other recent form of photo ID.

Types of IDs that are acceptable are: driver's license, marriage or divorce record, military record, employer ID card, adoption record, life insurance policy, passport, health insurance card, or school ID.

If you have any questions, call your local Social Security office or log on to www.socialsecurity.gov to find out what you need to know.

The Social Security application form asks you for certain information. Be sure that you know the answers to the following questions. Write the answers here, and make a copy to take with you to the Social Security office.

1. Your full name (the name you will use in work or business):

_____

2. Your name at birth: (This may be the same as or different from the name on line 1.)

_____

3. Your birthplace: _____

4. Your date of birth: _____

5. Your age at your last birthday: _____

6. Your mother's full name at birth: _____

7. Your father's full name at birth: _____

8. Your mailing address (include the zip code): _____

_____

9. Your area code and telephone number: _____

SKILL OBJECTIVES: Learning about Social Security; answering application form questions. Have students read the information, then ask: *Why do you need a Social Security number? Does anyone here have a number? When did you get it? When do you get money back from the Social Security system? How can you find out where the nearest Social Security office is? When you go to the office to apply for a number, what do you have to bring?* Have students complete the page independently. Provide help as needed.

Late Nate

Read the story. Then follow the instructions below it.

My friend, Nate, is late for school every morning. I stop at his house at 7:30, because we walk to the bus stop together. But he is never ready. He's still having breakfast or looking for his homework when I knock. I have to stand outside his door and wait while he rushes around trying to get his act together. Sometimes we miss the bus because Nate is late. Then his mother or father has to drive us to school. It's embarrassing. I tell Nate to wake up earlier. But it doesn't make any difference. If Nate gets up at 6:30, he's late. If Nate gets up at 6:00, he's late. No matter what he tries, he is always late for the bus! We are complete opposites, Nate and I. I am always on time. I am never, ever, late. I hate being late for school. But I like Nate. He is my best friend and a great guy. So I wait and wait for late Nate. It's the price of being his pal!

Now pretend that Nate was a friend of yours a few years ago. Write the story again, but change it from the present tense to the past tense. The first sentence is done for you.

My friend Nate was late for school every morning.

_____

_____

_____

_____

_____

_____

_____

_____

_____

_____

_____

_____

_____

_____

_____

SKILL OBJECTIVE: Using the simple past tense, regular and irregular forms. You may wish to cover this page as an oral group activity before assigning it for independent written work. Students may find sentences containing several verb phrases and/or contractions difficult to convert to the past tense.

Busy Body

Language Objectives
Define vocabulary. Answer questions about a reading. Make associations between movements and body parts.

A Make sure you know the meaning of the following important words which are underlined in the article.

internal	beats	filtering	blinking
messages	breathe	average	grows
pumps	liquid	destroyed	peels

B Read the article quickly to get some general ideas about it. Then read it again more slowly to answer the questions.

Body Works

Your body never stops. It works day and night. It works when you are awake and when you are asleep. It runs 24 hours a day, 8,760 hours a year. That's a busy body!

Your brain is the busiest part. It controls your <u>internal</u> body functions, all your thoughts, and all your movements. It sends out and receives more than a million <u>messages</u> a day. Even though your brain is in control, you are not consciously aware of a lot of the work your body does. There are so many things your brain takes care of automatically it's hard to keep count!

Your heart <u>pumps</u> about 3,000 gallons of blood each day. It <u>beats</u> around 100,000 times daily. You <u>breathe</u> about 23,000 times a day. Every breath you take brings in the oxygen you need and gets rid of carbon dioxide. Your stomach works to digest your food. It turns everything you eat into a <u>liquid</u> that then passes through your intestines. Your kidneys are constantly cleaning and <u>filtering</u> fluids that run through your body. On an <u>average</u> day, 250 million red blood cells in your body are

<u>destroyed</u> and replaced. The process of destroying and making new blood cells goes on around the clock. It's a full-time job to maintain the 20 trillion blood cells in your body. Your eyes are constantly <u>blinking</u> to keep them clean. Your hair <u>grows</u> about 2 hundredths of an inch every day. Your skin grows, too. Old cells peel off as new ones are made. An entire layer of your skin <u>peels</u> off and is replaced about every three weeks.

Of course, your body does lots of work that you are very aware of. You walk, run, jump, put on your clothes, go to class, play games, and so on. No wonder you are tired by the end of the day! All that work is exhausting. You need to sleep! But even when you sleep, your brain is active. You dream. And your body doesn't shut down completely. It is busy repairing itself while you rest. When you wake up, you are ready to go for another day!

Take care of your busy body. Eat right. Drink lots of water. Sleep well. Then your body will take care of you for a long time.

C Think carefully and answer the following question.

According to the article, you breathe about 23,000 times per day. Approximately how many times an hour do you breathe?

a. 12,000   **b.** 2,000   **c.** 1,000   **d.** 24

(Go on to the next page.)

SKILL OBJECTIVES: Identifying main idea and details; building vocabulary; making a mathematical calculation. Review the directions with the students. After the first reading, you may wish to lead a discussion about the meaning of the underlined vocabulary words. Encourage students to check and refine their definitions by using a dictionary.

D **What is the main idea of this article?**

    a. Your brain is the busiest part of your body.

    b. Millions of red blood cells are destroyed and replaced daily.

    c. Your body is constantly at work, when you are awake and when you sleep.

    d. Your skin peels off every three weeks.

E **Use a word from the underlined vocabulary list to complete each sentence.**

    1. Did you check your email _____ today?

    2. When ice melts, it turns from solid to _____ .

    3. Termites that eat wood have _____ that old house.

    4. David _____ vegetables in his backyard.

    5. Alicia _____ gasoline at the gas station.

F **Use the article to answer these questions. Give short answers.**

    1. About how many times does your heart beat each day? _____

    2. About how many red blood cells are destroyed and replaced daily? _____

    3. About how many red blood cells do you have? _____

    4. About how many messages does the brain send and receive each day? _____

    5. About how much does your hair grow each day? _____

G **Match each action with the body part that performs the action. Write the letter of the body part in the blank next to the action. Use a dictionary if you need to.**

    1. blink or wink   _____   **a.** ankle

    2. nod or shake   _____   **b.** tongue

    3. sniff or smell   _____   **c.** head

    4. lick or taste   _____   **d.** nose

    5. smile or whistle   _____   **e.** knee

    6. bite or chew   _____   **f.** mouth

    7. snap or cross   _____   **g.** eyes

    8. bend or kneel   _____   **h.** teeth

    9. sprain or twist   _____   **i.** fingers

    10. stub or wiggle   _____   **j.** toes

SKILL OBJECTIVES: Recalling details; building vocabulary. Students should complete these exercises independently. *Extension Activity:* Display a diagram of the organs in the human body. Have students locate the organs mentioned in this article: brain, heart, lungs, stomach, kidneys. Teach the names of other internal body parts and discuss their functions (veins, arteries, liver, intestines, etc.).

31

Word Skills: Adding -*ing*

When you write verbs in the present continuous and past continuous tenses, you use the ending -*ing*. Here are some rules to help you add that ending.

Language Objectives
Spell the -ing form of verbs correctly. Use -ing words correctly in sentences.

Rule 1:	For words that end in a silent (not pronounced) -*e*, drop the -*e* and add -*ing*.
	Example: smile → smiling
Rule 2:	For one-syllable words that end in consonant-vowel-consonant (except *x* and *w*), double the last letter and add -*ing*.
	Examples: sit → sitting run → running
Rule 3:	For most other words (including words that end in -*y*), add -*ing* with no changes.
	Examples: rain → raining send → sending

A Use these rules to add -*ing* to the following words:

1. shave	_____	**16.** hope	_____	**31.** save	_____
2. comb	_____	**17.** jump	_____	**32.** tap	_____
3. make	_____	**18.** joke	_____	**33.** carry	_____
4. feed	_____	**19.** marry	_____	**34.** buy	_____
5. do	_____	**20.** put	_____	**35.** sew	_____
6. empty	_____	**21.** say	_____	**36.** eat	_____
7. jog	_____	**22.** talk	_____	**37.** write	_____
8. take	_____	**23.** stop	_____	**38.** dream	_____
9. vacuum	_____	**24.** type	_____	**39.** cut	_____
10. go	_____	**25.** use	_____	**40.** roar	_____
11. sleep	_____	**26.** worry	_____	**41.** snap	_____
12. wax	_____	**27.** look	_____	**42.** dig	_____
13. change	_____	**28.** bat	_____	**43.** bury	_____
14. fry	_____	**29.** dance	_____	**44.** see	_____
15. get	_____	**30.** hurry	_____	**45.** skate	_____

B Now write a sentence in your notebook for each of the -*ing* words you made. If you wish, you may use more than one -*ing* word in a single sentence. For example:

While Dad was _____ing, Lee was _____ing on the telephone, and I was upstairs _____ing.

SKILL OBJECTIVES: Constructing gerunds; applying rules for spelling changes. Review the rules for spelling changes with the class. Do several examples together, then assign the page for independent written work. After Part B has been completed, ask each student to read his/her favorite sentence aloud to the class.

Thank You

Language Objective
Thank a person by writing a thank-you note.

When someone gives you something, you say "Thank you." Sometimes, however, a letter or note is expected. Thank-you notes are usually sent:

- when someone sends you a gift—for example, a birthday or Christmas present

- when you have visited someone—for example, for a weekend or a vacation

Here are two different kinds of thank-you notes:

February 8

Dear Carolina,

   The scarf you sent to me is just beautiful. It's just the color I needed to go with my gray coat, and it's so soft!
   Thank you so much. It was sweet of you to remember my birthday.

love,
Lucy

May 16

Dear Anh,

   I had a wonderful time at your home last weekend. I was a little nervous at first, but everyone was so friendly. I felt right at home.
   Thank you very much for having me.

Sincerely,
Ngoc

Notice that the notes are short and that they are written by hand, not typewritten. Thank-you notes should be sent promptly—within a month for gifts, and within a week after your return for visits.

Practice writing a thank-you note. Use the space below. Write your note to an aunt who has just sent you a sweater for your birthday. Or, if you have just received a gift or come back from a visit, write a note thanking the person who gave you the gift or asked you to visit.

_____

_____

_____

_____

_____

_____

SKILL OBJECTIVE: Writing a thank–you note. Read and discuss the information on this page with the class. Draw attention to the opening (*Dear …*) and closing (*Love,* or *Sincerely,*) used in a friendly letter. Have students note the indention used. The date is often written in the upper right-hand corner; the closing is then aligned with the date. Circulate around the room as students write their notes, offering help as needed.

Dear Dot

Dear Dot,

I am very angry with my children. Six weeks ago they found a puppy and brought it home. They promised me that they were going to feed it and walk it and take care of it. It was so little and cute that I decided they could keep it, even though I don't like dogs very much. Here's my problem: No one takes care of the puppy. I walk it every day. I feed it and clean up after it. No one else can seem to find the time. Dot, I am busy, too, and I don't want to be responsible for this dog. What can I do?

Fido's Nursemaid

1. Who is angry with the children? _____

2. What did the children promise? _____
_____

3. What does Nursemaid do every day? _____
_____

4. Why doesn't anyone else take care of the dog? _____
_____

5. What does the word *promised* in this letter mean? Circle the best answer.

   a. lied   **b.** broke   **c.** stole   **d.** assured

6. What is your advice to Fido's Nursemaid? Discuss your answer in class. Then read Dot's answer and tell why you agree or disagree. Dot's advice is below.

Dear Nursemaid,

Remind your children about their promise to take care of the dog. After supper, keep them at the table until they complete a schedule, showing when each one is going to be responsible for the puppy. If anyone misses a day, give him or her extra chores to do around the house. Tell them that if they don't cooperate, you might have to take the dog to the pound—and remind them about what happens there.

Dot

Write About It

In your notebook, make a list of rules or write a paragraph that explains the responsibilities of owning a pet.

SKILL OBJECTIVES: Reading for details; drawing conclusions; understanding words through context; making judgments. Have students read the letter and answer the questions independently. Students can write their advice to "Fido's Nursemaid" in their notebooks. Correct the first five questions as a class, then have students compare and discuss their own advice and Dot's reply. You may wish to assign the "Write About It" topic as homework.

The Present Perfect Tense (1)

The present perfect tense is used to tell about something that happened at an unspecified time in the past. To form the present perfect, use *have* or *has* with the past participle of the main verb. Look at these examples with *eat*.

| I You We They | } have eaten. | He She It | } has eaten. |

Present perfect (unspecified time):
    I have eaten there twice.
Past (specified time):
    I ate there last night.

A Use *have/has* and the past participle (see Data Bank) to complete these sentences. The first one is done for you.

1. Carlos (be) _____*has been*_____ to Chicago three times.
2. Mary and Bob (go) _____ to Miami often.
3. I (eat) _____ at that restaurant twice.
4. It (snow) _____ twice so far this winter.
5. Susan (read) _____ that book before.
6. My cousins (see) _____ that movie several times.

DATA BANK

| ~~been~~ | eaten | gone | read | seen | snowed |

B Write the past participle form of the verbs below. If the verb is regular *(-ed)* in the past form, it is also regular *(-ed)* in the past participle form. The present and past forms of each verb are given; you fill in the past participle. Refer to pages 113 and 114 if you need to. The first two are done for you.

1. apply / applied	*applied*	15. find / found	
2. begin / began	*begun*	16. get / got	
3. break / broke		17. give / gave	
4. bring / brought		18. have / had	
5. buy / bought		19. increase / increased	
6. call / called		20. keep / kept	
7. choose / chose		21. know / knew	
8. come / came		22. leave / left	
9. cost / cost		23. live / lived	
10. decide / decided		24. lose / lost	
11. do / did		25. make / made	
12. drive / drove		26. meet / met	
13. enjoy / enjoy		27. move / moved	
14. fall / fell		28. pay / paid	

SKILL OBJECTIVES: Using the present perfect tense; forming regular and irregular past participles. Introduce/review the construction and use of the present perfect tense. Read the material at the top of the page and explain the difference between "specified" and "unspecified." *Part A:* Do the items orally together. Then assign for independent written work. *Part B:* See how many past participles students can fill in without referring to pages 113–114. Then have them use these pages to complete the others.

The Present Perfect Tense (2)

Language Objective
Distinguish between the simple past and the present perfect tense by answering and asking questions.

A The president of a large company has to travel to different countries on business. Here is a list of countries she has visited since 2000 when she became president.

2000	2002	2003
February: Spain	January: Japan	February: Brazil
May: England	March: Mexico	April: Spain
June: Japan	July: Italy	May: Canada
September: Brazil	August: Canada	August: Japan
October: Mexico	November: China	December: Mexico

Use the information above to answer these questions. Answer in complete sentences. The first ones are done for you.

1. How many times has the president been to _____?

   a. Spain _____She's been to Spain twice._____

   b. Japan _____

   c. Italy _____

   d. Mexico _____

2. When did the president go to?

   a. Canada _____She went to Canada in 2002 and 2003._____

   b. Italy _____

   c. Brazil _____

   d. China _____

B Look at the box showing different uses of the present perfect tense.

Affirmative:	I have been to New York twice.
Negative:	I have never been to Spain.
Question:	Have you ever been to Canada?

What about you? Answer in a complete sentence. The first two are examples.

1. Have you ever eaten at Café Flavio? _____Yes, I have eaten there many times._____

2. Have you ever ridden a horse? _____No, I have never ridden a horse._____

3. Have you ever used a computer? _____

4. Have you ever played polo? _____

5. Have you ever been to a wedding? _____

6. Have you ever moved? _____

SKILL OBJECTIVE: Using the present perfect and past tenses. Review the construction and use of the present perfect tense. *Part A:* Have volunteers read the months and places the president visited in 2000, 2002, and 2003. Call attention to the first question. What tense is used? Why? Have students complete 1b, 1c, and 1d. Then have them look at 2a. What tense is used? Why? Have them complete Part A. *Part B:* Have volunteers read the three sentences in the box aloud. Go through the first two questions orally, then assign the others for independent written work.

Have You Ever?

Language Objectives
Ask and record information about various activities.
Write an essay using recorded information.

A Interview three of your classmates to get answers for the ten questions below. Make notes of each student's responses on the chart.

Name:	Name:	Name:

1. Have you ever eaten dinner at midnight? When?

2. Have you ever met a famous person? Who?

3. Have you ever found money in the street? How much?

4. Have you ever cooked dinner for your family? What?

5. Have you ever been to Disney World? When?

6. Have you ever slept until noon? How often?

7. Have you ever had a job? What?

8. Have you ever been in the hospital? When? Why?

9. Have you ever traveled by plane? Where?

10. Have you ever tried Italian food? What?

B Use the results of your interviews to write a paragraph about your classmates. Use more paper if you need to. The first sentence is done for you.

My classmates have done many interesting things.

_____

_____

_____

_____

SKILL OBJECTIVES: Using the present perfect tense; interviewing; writing an informative paragraph. Have a student interview first you, then several classmates with the first few questions. Model the correct answer structures. Show how to note the essential information on the interview chart. Point out the use of simple past *vs.* present perfect. Note that the second question is asked only if the first answer is *yes.* Provide as much group practice as needed, then have students form pairs and interview each other.

Reading a Map

This is a map of part of the Rapid Transit lines of the Massachusetts Bay Transportation Authority (MBTA). The MBTA runs most public transportation in Boston and surrounding cities. This map shows the Rapid Transit lines in downtown Boston. Notice that there are four lines, called the Red, Green, Orange, and Blue lines. The map also shows some of the places that are near the stations on the four lines.

A Use the map to answer the questions below. Use more paper if you need to. Be sure your answers are complete. The first one is done for you.

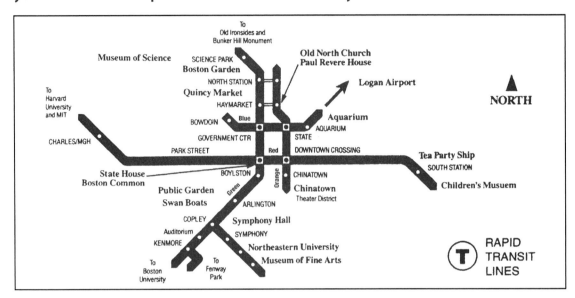

1. Using the MBTA, how can you get from Chinatown to the Aquarium?

   Take the Orange Line north to the second stop (State). Get on the

   Blue Line east and take it to the first stop.

2. How can you get from the Museum of Science to the Museum of Fine Arts? _____

   _____

3. How can you get from the Aquarium to Symphony Hall? _____

   _____

4. How can you get from the Public Garden to Chinatown? _____

   _____

5. How can you get from Quincy Market to Downtown Crossing? _____

   _____

B In your notebook, write directions to get to a "mystery stop" on the MBTA. Tell where to start, which line or lines to take, and how many stops to travel. Have a classmate read your directions and see if he or she reaches your "mystery stop."

SKILL OBJECTIVES: Interpreting a transit map; writing and following written directions. Read the introductory paragraph with the class. Have students trace the four lines. Call attention to the north-pointing arrowhead and review the directions north, south, east, and west. *Part A:* Work through the first question with the class and have them trace the route. Then assign the others for independent written work. Correct the questions orally with the group. *Part B:* Have students work independently to write their directions. Then have them work in pairs, giving each other the directions. You may want to have several volunteers read their directions to the class.

The Water Cycle

Read the article.

Language Objective
Interpret and complete a chart about a scientific process.

Water is everywhere. More than three-fourths of the Earth is covered by water. Our bodies are mostly water. We must drink water to survive. We swim in it, wash in it, cook with it, and travel on it. Plants and animals depend on water, too. Water is essential to all life.

What is water? It is a compound made up of two elements: hydrogen (H) and oxygen (O). Hydrogen and oxygen are gases. When they bond together they make H_2O, or water, which is a liquid.

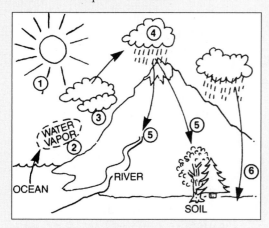

Water formed on the earth billions of years ago. This water has been recycled over and over again. The process is simple. Water evaporates and then precipitates. That means water goes up into the air as vapor and comes back down again as rain or snow. This process of evaporating and precipitating is called the water cycle. The diagram shows how it works. Use the dictionary to look up words you don't know.

1. The sun heats water in the oceans, lakes, and rivers.
2. Some of the water turns into water vapor. Water vapor rises into the air. This is evaporation.
3. The water vapor cools and condenses intowater droplets. This is how clouds are made.
4. Water in clouds falls back to the earth as rain or snow. This is precipitation.
5. Rain may fall directly into the oceans, lakes, and rivers completing the cycle.
6. Rain may fall on the land. Rainwater and melted snow flow into streams and rivers that flow into the ocean to be recycled again.
7. Rainwater can filter through the soil. Wells and springs can bring this water back to the surface. Eventually, this water may flow to the ocean.

A **Look at the numbered diagram of the water cycle above. Fill in each numbered blank below to describe how the water cycle works.**

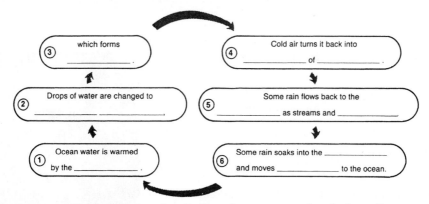

B **Do you live near an ocean, lake, or river? If so, in your notebook describe your feelings about the water you live near. Describe how people in your community use the water. If you do not live near water, describe your feelings about it. Would you like to be near water or not? Why?**

SKILL OBJECTIVES: Identifying main ideas and details; interpreting and completing a chart. Have students read the article quickly to get a general idea of the subject. Ask, *What is this article about?* (topic) Have students identify unfamiliar words. Help them use context clues to discover approximate meanings. Have students reread the text, then describe the water cycle to a partner, using the diagram as a prop. Have students complete Part A independently or with a partner. Part B may be assigned as homework.

The Declaration of Independence

A Make sure you know the meaning of the following important words which are underlined in the article.

document	equal	interfering	accusations	protected
created	preventing	simplified	forced	refused

B Read the article quickly to get some general ideas about it. Then read it again more slowly to answer the questions.

An Important Document

The Declaration of Independence is an important <u>document</u> in the history of the United States. Thomas Jefferson is the author of this great work. He wrote it long before he was President of the United States. The first part of the Declaration of Independence says that all men are <u>created</u> <u>equal</u> and that they have a right to life, liberty, and happiness. In the second part of the Declaration, Jefferson explained that the King of England was <u>preventing</u> the colonists from having these rights.

To show the world exactly how the King was <u>interfering</u> with the freedoms of the colonists, Thomas Jefferson included in the Declaration of Independence a long list of the King's policies in the colonies. Here is a shortened and <u>simplified</u> list of the <u>accusations</u> Thomas Jefferson made against the King of England.

1. He has taxed us against our wishes.
2. He has deprived us of our rights.
3. He has ordered British soldiers into our homes.
4. He has burned our towns.
5. He has <u>forced</u> Americans to serve in the British navy.
6. He has helped the Indians to attack western villages.
7. He has <u>protected</u> British soldiers who have murdered innocent colonists.
8. He has closed down some of our Houses of Representatives.
9. He has <u>refused</u> to let us have elections.
10. He has passed laws that have hurt the American people.

Thomas Jefferson ended the Declaration of Independence by saying that the thirteen colonies were no longer part of the British Empire. They did not belong to the King anymore. The colonies were now the United States of America. They were a new nation in a new world.

C Think carefully and answer the following question.

What did the King of England most likely think about the U.S. Declaration of Independence?

a. He agreed with it completely.

b. He liked some parts of it.

c. He was angry about it and disagreed with it.

d. He thought the colonists had some good ideas.

(Go on to the next page.)

Thomas Jefferson

SKILL OBJECTIVES: Reading comprehension; building vocabulary. Review the directions with the students. After the first reading, you may want to lead a discussion about the meaning of the highlighted vocabulary words. Encourage students to check and refine their definitions by using a dictionary.

D Often you can *draw a conclusion* from something you read. That is, you can figure out the answer to a question even though that answer is not stated in the reading. Draw a conclusion to complete the following sentence. Circle your answer.

The colonists wanted to be independent because

a. all men are created equal.

b. the King treated them unfairly.

c. they wanted to be the United States of America.

d. all men have a right to liberty and happiness.

E Use a word from the underlined vocabulary to complete each of the sentences.

1. The work was too hard for the students, so the teacher _____ it.

2. The waiter cut the cake into six _____ pieces.

3. The striking workers shouted _____ in front of the factory.

4. I asked my boss for a raise but he _____ to give it to me.

5. Many politicians signed their names to this _____.

F Write the answers to these questions in your notebook.

1. Who is the author of the Declaration of Independence?

2. What rights do all Americans have, according to the Declaration?

3. Who was keeping these rights from the colonists?

4. How did Thomas Jefferson end the Declaration of Independence?

5. What was the new name for the American colonies?

G Find details in the article that best complete the following outline.

The Declaration of Independence

A. The Introduction (the first part)

1. _____

2. _____

B. The Accusations Against the King

1. _____

2. _____

3. _____

4. _____

5. _____

C. The Conclusion (the ending)

1. _____

2. _____

SKILL OBJECTIVES: Drawing conclusions; recalling details; building vocabulary; completing an outline. Students should complete the exercises independently. In Part G, Section B, they may choose any five of the accusations listed against the king. *Extension Activity:* Looking at a U.S. map, have students guess the thirteen colonies that signed the Declaration. (NH, MA, RI, CT, NY, NJ, DE, PA, MD, VA, NC, SC, GA.) Have students count the red and white stripes on the U.S. flag. Note that these stripes represent the original thirteen states.

Word Skills: Adding -ed

Language Objectives
Complete a chart with the missing verb forms. Write sentences that use past tense or past participles correctly.

When you write the past tense and the past participle of regular verbs, you use the ending -ed. Here are some rules to help you add that ending.

Rule 1:	For words that already end in -e, simply add the letter d.
	Examples: love → loved like → liked
Rule 2:	For words that end in a consonant followed by y, change the y to i and add -ed.
	Examples: marry → married hurry → hurried
Rule 3:	For most words that end in a vowel followed by y, simply add -ed with no changes.
	Examples: play → played stay → stayed
Rule 4:	For one-syllable words that end in consonant-vowel-consonant (except x), double the last letter and add -ed. (Note: Never double final x.)
	Examples: stop → stopped jog → jogged
Rule 5:	For most other words (including words that end in x), simply add -ed with no changes.
	Examples: wish → wished enter → entered
Rule 6:	Irregular verbs. There is no rule you can follow when you write the past participle forms of *irregular* verbs. You have to memorize them.

A Use these rules to form words in the chart below. Use pages 113–114 for help if you need to. The first two rows are done for you.

Present	Past	Past Participle
walk	walked	walked
go	went	gone
	rode	
		visited
speak		
	thought	
practice		
		written
play		
	built	
win		
	spent	
save		
	worried	
		married

B Now write a sentence in your notebook for each of the past or past participle words in the chart. If you wish, you may use more than one of these words in a single sentence. For example:

She practiced her speech before she spoke to the class.

SKILL OBJECTIVES: Forming present, past, and past participle forms; observing spelling changes. *Part A:* Go over the six rules together. Work through the first two rows as a class. Be sure students understand why they have been completed as they have. Then assign the remaining rows as independent work. See how many each student can complete without having to consult pages 113–114, but allow them to refer to these pages to finish Part A. *Part B:* You may wish to limit the number of sentences to those where students had to fill in the second or third column. Be sure the present perfect tense is used correctly in sentences using the past participle.

What Have They Done?

Language Objective
Use context clues to tell
what someone has done.

Read each of the following stories. Tell what the people have done. Use the Data Bank to help you with the past participles, but answer each question in a complete sentence. The first one is done for you.

1. Miguel is very happy as he walks into the house. He is waving a pink certificate in the air. He shouts, "I got it! I got it!" He says, "Now I can drive to work, to school, and on dates."

   What has Miguel done? _He has gotten his license._

2. Mary opens the envelope slowly. She takes out the report card. "I don't dare look at my history grade," she says. Finally she looks. "It's a C," she says joyfully. "I won't have to go to summer school."

   What has Mary done? _____

3. Trang rereads her pages. She types the footnotes and the bibliography. "It took more than a month, but it's finished," she says to herself happily.

   What has Trang done? _____

4. Marc and Oscar come late to work for the third time in a week. Mr. Carmiletti, their boss, sees them. At the end of the shift, he calls them to the office. "Boys, don't come back in tomorrow. You're fired," he tells them.

   What have the boys done? _____

5. Connie and Joanne come in from outside. "We have plenty of fresh ingredients for tonight's salad," says Joanne. "It's all from our own garden," says Connie.

   What have they done? _____

6. "No wonder we're lost," says Mrs. Ramirez, looking up from the directions. "You took Exit 23, and we were supposed to take Exit 32." "We'd better get back on the Interstate, I guess," says Mr. Ramirez.

   What has Mr. Ramirez done? _____

7. The Wilson twins are six years old and they feel very proud of themselves. Their mother was napping, and they did a chore without her asking. They put the plates, knives, forks, spoons, and napkins out for dinner.

   What have the children done? _____

8. Mr. Li looks at the clock. It is 6:15, but he doesn't have to get up this morning. He has been going to work for forty years, but last Friday was his last day on the job. He's going to take it easy and spend more time with his family.

   What has Mr. Li done? _____

DATA BANK

picked (lettuce and tomatoes)	passed (the course)	retired (from his job)
~~gotten (his license)~~	written (her term paper)	taken (the wrong turn)
lost (their jobs)	set (the table)	

SKILL OBJECTIVES: Predicting outcomes; reviewing present perfect tense. Explain unfamiliar words. Have students work in pairs to come up with correct answer. Be sure students write complete sentences. You may wish to make this page a contest, with the winners being the first pair to finish with correct answers.

43

Dear Dot

Dear Dot,

My father is a grouch. When he comes home, he never says "hello" or asks how I am. Instead he says, "Have you done your homework? Or "Have you cleaned your room?" His other favorite question is "Have you emptied the trash?" His first question to my mother is, "Have you cooked dinner yet?" After dinner he isn't quite as grouchy, but he's never in a really good mood. I can't stand much more of his grouchiness. I have thought of getting my own apartment, but I am only sixteen and still in school. What can I do?

Donna

1. What questions does Donna's father ask her when he comes home? _____

_____

2. What question does he ask her mother? _____

_____

3. When is Donna's father less grouchy? _____

_____

4. What has Donna thought of doing? _____

_____

5. What does the word *mood* in this letter mean? Circle the best answer.

    a. room   **b.** state of mind   **c.** verb   **d.** change of heart

6. What is your advice to Donna? Discuss your answer in class. Then take Dot's role and write your answer to Donna's letter. Tell her what to do and what not to do.

    Dear Donna, _____

_____

_____

_____

_____

_____

_____

_____

SKILL OBJECTIVES: Reading for details; drawing conclusions; making judgments; writing a letter. Have students read the letter and answer questions 1–5 independently. Correct these as a class. Then have students discuss question 6 and write their letters. Have several volunteers read their letters and have the class make suggestions for rephrasing, etc. As an additional option, ask students to write a descriptive paragraph about a happy person, telling what he or she looks like and what his or her attitude toward life is. (Students may be the subjects of their own paragraphs if they are that kind of person.)

44

Can You? Could You?

Language Objective
Answer questions using <u>can</u>, <u>can't</u>, <u>could</u>, <u>couldn't</u>.

A Answer these questions. The first two are done for you. Use them as models.

1. Can you speak English?   <u>Yes, I can.</u>

2. Could you speak English last summer? <u>No, I couldn't.</u>

3. Can you ride a horse?   _____

4. Could you find your shoes this morning? _____

5. Can you type?   _____

6. Could you tell time when you were four years old? _____

B Complete the sentence with *can, can't, could,* or *couldn't.* The first one is done for you.

1. Today, girls ____<u>can</u>____ take an auto mechanics course in most high schools. Forty years ago, girls _____ take this course in most schools.

2. If you are not an American citizen, you _____ vote for President.

3. A fast runner, like Margarita, _____ run more than five miles in half an hour.

4. As a boy, Mr. Ruiz was a good football player. He _____ play very well.

5. Pam and Sam _____ go to the beach yesterday because it was raining hard.

6. Emily Yee lives in San Francisco. On sunny days, she _____ see the Golden Gate Bridge from her window, but on foggy days she _____.

7. If you use the Yellow Pages, you _____ find the number of a hospital.

8. Because Beethoven was deaf, he _____ hear the last symphonies he wrote.

9. There was a lot of snow last winter, so Kevin _____ go skiing often.

10. Forty years ago in most high schools, boys _____ take a cooking course, but now they _____ take one.

11. I like to listen to music, but I _____ play the piano at all.

12. Carmen is blind now, but when she was young, she _____ see very well.

SKILL OBJECTIVE: Using modals *can/can't, could/couldn't.* Teach/review the modals by asking students questions and writing on the board: *Could you walk on your hands two years ago? Can you walk on your hands now? Can you name ten states? Could you do your math homework last night?* Assign the page for independent written work. *Extension Activity:* Have students complete these sentences any way they like: *…years ago, I couldn't…, but I can now. …years ago, I could …, but I can't now.*

Inventors

Language Objectives
Define vocabulary. Answer questions about a reading. Combine clauses using context clues to make complex sentences.

A Make sure you know the meaning of the following important words which are underlined in the article.

inventors	phonograph	electricity	dynamo	patents
genius	dictating	network	equipment	copier

B Read the article quickly to get some general ideas about it. Then read it again more slowly to answer the questions.

Two Amazing Minds

The United States has produced many great <u>inventors</u>. The most famous is Thomas Edison. He was a real <u>genius</u>. He invented over 1,000 items. Among his inventions are the electric vote recorder, <u>phonograph</u>, movie camera, and <u>dictating</u> machine. Edison perfected the electric light bulb in 1879. But no one could use it! Houses did not have <u>electricity</u>! Only scientists used electricity in their labs. In order to bring electricity to the public, Edison and his workers had to make an electrical <u>network</u> that was safe and affordable. First, Edison had to build a <u>dynamo</u>, or generator, to make the electricity. Wires to carry the electricity from the generator into homes had to be installed. Wiring and sockets had to be placed in homes.

Edison decided to electrify America's largest city, New York, first! He made all the machines and <u>equipment</u> he needed for this massive task. By 1887, much of New York had electricity. Edison's company was named the Edison Electric Light Company. This company supplied electricity to New York and many other places that wanted it for years to come.

Edison's many inventions helped America take a giant step forward into the twentieth century.

One of the most successful women inventors was Beulah Henry. She was born in 1887, about the time Edison was electrifying New York City. Beulah Henry is sometimes called a "Lady Edison." She invented 110 items and had forty-nine <u>patents</u> in her name. She did this at a time when women held less than one per cent of the patents granted in the United States. Ms. Henry invented clever toys and games for children. She also invented a machine to make ice cream, a new kind of sewing machine, and a kind of <u>copier</u> that didn't use carbon paper. One of her inventions was a changeable umbrella. People could change the material on their umbrellas to match their clothes.

Beulah Henry has been a role model for women inventors. Since the early half of the twentieth century, women have been inventing things and earning patents at a much higher rate. Today, some twenty per cent of all patents in the United States are granted to women.

C Think carefully and answer the following question.

What happened after Edison electrified New York City?

a. Other cities wanted electricity, too.

b. People who wanted electricity moved to New York.

c. Thomas Edison went out of business.

d. World War II began.

(Go on to the next page.)

SKILL OBJECTIVES: Reading comprehension; making inferences; building vocabulary. Review the directions with the students. After the first reading, you may wish to lead a discussion about the meaning of the highlighted vocabulary words. Encourage students to check and refine their definitions by using a dictionary.

D Draw a conclusion from the article to complete the following sentence. Circle your answer.

Inventors in the United States

- **a.** invented everything.
- **b.** all study at a university.
- **c.** are men and women.
- **d.** make umbrellas.

E Use a word from the underlined vocabulary to complete each of these sentences.

1. Mozart was a musical _____.
2. The CD player replaced the _____.
3. That car doesn't use gas. It runs on _____.
4. The blind novelist was _____ a new novel to his assistant.
5. We use exercise _____ in gym class.

F Write the answers to these questions in your notebook.

1. How many items did Thomas Edison invent?
2. How many items did Beulah Henry invent?
3. What are some of Edison's inventions?
4. What are some of Henry's inventions?
5. What was the first city in America to have electricity?
6. What was Edison's company called?
7. Why do you think Edison's inventions were important to America?
8. Why was Beulah Henry an important inventor?
9. Today what percentage of inventors are men?
10. What is your favorite invention? Why?

Thomas Edison

G Match the beginnings of the sentences at the left with their endings at the right. Write the letter of the correct ending in the blank.

1. People read by candle, gas, or oil _____	**a.** until Judson Whitcomb invented the zipper.
2. People studied the stars with the naked eye _____	**b.** until Alfred Nobel invented dynamite.
3. People wrote letters by hand _____	**c.** until Elisha Otis invented the elevator.
4. People made ice cream by hand _____	**d.** until Beulah Henry invented the ice cream maker.
5. People blasted open mines with gunpowder _____	**e.** until Thomas Edison invented the light bulb.
6. People walked up stairs in buildings _____	**f.** until Johannes Kepler invented the astronomical telescope.
7. People fastened their clothing with buttons _____	**g.** until Christopher Sholes invented the typewriter.

SKILL OBJECTIVES: Reading for details; drawing conclusions; building vocabulary; determining cause and effect. Students should complete the page independently. *Extension Activity*: Encourage students to research the inventor and dates of the following inventions. Students should look in one or more encyclopedias, then report their findings to the class: *chewing gum, ballpoint pen, ferris wheel, frozen food, safety pin, barbed wire, roller skates, watches, saxophone, margarine.*

Do You Have To?

Language Objective
Complete sentences and ask and answer questions using the correct form of <u>have to</u>.

A Complete the following sentences by using *have to, has to,* or *had to.* The first one is done for you.

1. Carla ___has to___ study tonight.

2. My parents _____ pay a lot of bills every month.

3. You _____ take Physics I before you can take Physics II.

4. Lisa couldn't attend the meeting because she _____ visit her mother in the hospital.

5. My mother said I _____ vacuum the living room before I could go to the ball game.

6. My grandfather _____ weed his garden every week.

7. Mr. and Mrs. Ruiz _____ move to a different apartment after the fire destroyed their building.

8. Does Vuong _____ walk the dog when he gets home?

9. John's grandfather _____ wear his glasses when he reads the newspaper.

10. Did you _____ call the doctor about your problem?

11. You _____ insure the package before you mail it.

12. I _____ go to the doctor for a checkup yesterday.

B Excuses, Excuses! Think of three good excuses for each of the following situations. Use *had to* or *have to.* The first one is done for you. Use it as a model.

Why didn't you do your homework?

1. ___I had to cook dinner for my family.___

2. _____

3. _____

Why can't you help me with the housework?

1. _____

2. _____

3. _____

Why couldn't Carla come to my party?

1. She _____

2. _____

3. _____

SKILL OBJECTIVE: Using *have to, has to, had to.* Ask several students questions. Write their responses on the board. *What do you have to do after school today? What did you have to do last weekend?* Then ask their classmates: *What does (Ana) have to do today? What do (Raul and Lars) have to do? What did … have to do last week?* Assign Part A for independent written work. Students may work on Part B in pairs. Encourage students to share their excuses with their classmates.

Word Skills: Synonyms

Language Objective
Replace common words in sentences with an appropriate synonym.

Words that have the same or nearly the same meaning are called synonyms. *Leave* and *depart* are synonyms because they mean the same thing.

Example: The bus *leaves* at 3:00.
The bus *departs* at 3:00.

Read each sentence. Find a synonym for the underlined word in the Data Bank at the bottom of the page and write it on the line following the sentence. The first one is done for you.

1. The car isn't working; Felix is trying to <u>fix</u> it. *repair*

2. Lorenzo's books are downstairs in the <u>basement</u>. _____

3. The scouts are going camping in the <u>forest</u> this weekend. _____

4. The houses on this <u>road</u> are beautiful. _____

5. Class is going to <u>start</u> in ten minutes. _____

6. The library is going to show a French <u>movie</u> this afternoon. _____

7. This shirt was very <u>cheap</u>; I got it on sale. _____

8. The teacher told the children not to act <u>silly</u>. _____

9. Ilhan exercises every day; he feels <u>great</u>. _____

10. My friend hasn't answered my letter; I'm <u>nervous</u> about that. _____

11. Larry was <u>sad</u> when his vacation was over. _____

12. Lucio is emptying the <u>trash</u> this week. _____

13. Please <u>close</u> the door when you leave. _____

14. Please don't <u>talk</u> to me when I am driving. _____

15. The boys have to <u>hurry</u> because they are late. _____

16. Mr. Chin was <u>angry</u> about losing his watch. _____

17. Tom's <u>home</u> is a very comfortable place to be. _____

18. Everyone in the club was <u>happy</u> to meet Professor Klein. _____

19. Chipmunks and mice are <u>little</u> animals. _____

20. New York and Los Angeles are <u>big</u> cities. _____

DATA BANK

begin	cellar	film	foolish	garbage	glad	house
inexpensive	large	mad	~~repair~~	rush	shut	small
speak	street	unhappy	wonderful	woods	worried	

SKILL OBJECTIVE: Identifying synonyms. Go over the directions with the class, then complete the first few items together. Assign the page as independent written work. *Extension Activity*: Review the definition of *antonym* (page 21). Have students create a chart listing first a synonym and then an antonym for each of the following words: *terrible, skinny, enjoy, difficult, grin, begin, yell, quick.*

49

By Myself

A Complete each sentence with one of the following *reflexive* pronouns.

myself	yourself	himself	herself	itself	ourselves	yourselves	themselves

1. Alex lives by _____.

2. Even though Anna is only three years old, she can dress _____.

3. Rembrandt painted many pictures of _____.

4. We are cooking up a feast for _____ today!

5. Class, you should be proud of _____!

6. You can make your bed by _____.

7. Manuel is old enough to walk to school by _____.

8. Marie Curie made a name for _____ in the field of science.

9. I knitted _____ a beautiful sweater.

10. Charles Lindbergh crossed the ocean by _____.

11. The fire in the trashcan burned _____ out in a few seconds.

12. Grace and Juana designed the set _____.

13. I'm setting new goals for _____.

14. We bought _____ a new fish tank.

15. Paula found the strength within _____ to win.

B Complete each sentence with the correct subject pronoun.

I	you	he	she	it	we	they

1. _____ can do the laundry all by myself.

2. _____ built the garage himself.

3. _____ threw ourselves a party.

4. _____ outdoes herself every day.

5. _____ should give yourself a pat on the back!

6. _____ trust myself to make a good decision.

7. _____ have to see the movie yourself.

8. _____ planned the trip themselves.

9. _____ cleaned up the kitchen by myself.

10. _____ got ourselves a puppy.

SKILL OBJECTIVE: Reviewing subject and reflexive pronouns. Complete the first few items as a group, then assign for independent written work. Correct as a class.

What's on TV?

Here is part of the television program for one evening in a large city area. Use the program to answer the questions. The first one is done for you.

Language Objective
Answer questions about a TV schedule.

7:00
- ❑ Dateline/Is the Atkins Diet safe?. 2
- ❑ NBC News 4
- ❑ ABC News 5
- ❑ Extra 6
- ❑ Wheel of Fortune. . . 7-12
- ❑ Access Hollywood. . . 10
- ❑ Movie: Brad Pitt in "Troy". 2:00 25
- ❑ Nightly Business Report/Market updates and indepth economic news 36-44
- ❑ Frasier/Martin's wedding causes tumult. 38
- ❑ Hope & Faith/Faith has received an Emmy nomination 56
- ❑ Friends/Monica and Chandler get married . . 58
- ❑ Star Trek/"The Trouble with Tribbles" Ravenous, furry tribbles, irate officials, and hostile Klingons complicate an Enterprise cargo delivery. 1:00 . . . 64
- ❑ Biography/Mary J. Blige . . . . A&E
- ❑ Movie/"The Richest Girl in the World" (2004) a remake of the 1934 Joel McCrea hit. 1:30. . . . . AMC
- ❑ Larry King Live/Bob Woodward. . . . . CNN
- ❑ SportsCenter. . . . . ESPN
- ❑ Providence/Syd helps Joanie's friend. 1:00. . LIFE
- ❑ Red Sox Digest. . . . NESN
- ❑ Rugrats. . . . . NICK
- ❑ JAG 1:00. . . . . USA
- ❑ Sports Nightly. . . . . FOX

7:30
- ❑ Bob Vila/Bob uses a lathe and router to make a candle stand. 2
- ❑ Hollywood Squares. . . 4
- ❑ 20/20/A look at young royalty in the 21st century. 5
- ❑ The Bachelor. 6
- ❑ Entertainment Tonight 10
- ❑ Extra. 25
- ❑ Law & Order/Special Victims Unit. 38
- ❑ Newshour with Jim Lehrer. 44

- ❑ The Simpsons/Bart and family go to Paris. 56
- ❑ Movie/"The Bell Jar" (1979) Marilyn Hassett, Julie Harris. 2:30 58
- ❑ American Justice . . . A&E
- ❑ Baseball Tonight . . . ESPN
- ❑ Wimbledon '04 Highlights . . . . HBO
- ❑ Garth Brooks in concert. . . . . NASH
- ❑ Baseball/Milwaukee Brewers at Boston Red Sox. (Live) . . . . NESN
- ❑ SpongeBob SquarePants . . . . . . NICK
- ❑ Horse Racing/ "Rockingham Report". FOX
- ❑ King of Queens. . WWOR

8:00
- ❑ This Old House/Exterior painting; plastering; a security system. 2
- ❑ Seinfeld/A self-help guru praises Jerry. 4-10
- ❑ Baseball/Cincinnati Reds at New York Mets. (Live) 5-12
- ❑ 60 Minutes/"Tell Me a Story" is reviewed. 1:00 6-7
- ❑ Movie/"52 Pick-Up" (1986) Roy Scheider, Ann-Margret. 2:00 25
- ❑ Reba/Reba prepares for a 5K race 36
- ❑ Movie/"Dragnet" (1954) Jack Webb, Ben Alexander. 2:00 38
- ❑ Capitol Report/American business in China. 68
- ❑ Durrell in Russia/Gerald and Lee Durrell examine wildlife of Russia, starting with a visit to the Moscow Zoo. . . . . A&E
- ❑ Movie/"Return to Waterloo" (1985) Ken Colley, Valerie Holliman. 1:00 . . . . BRAVO
- ❑ Movie/"Johnny Holiday" (1949) William Bendix, Allen Martin Jr. 2:00. . . . . .CBN
- ❑ Walt Disney Presents/"A Disney Vacation" . . . . . DIS

- ❑ Auto Racing/"Corvette Challenge Series." From Detroit . . . . ESPN
- ❑ Movie/"The Great Outdoors" (1988) Dan Aykroyd, John Candy. 1:30 . . . . .HBO
- ❑ Movie/"The Don is Dead" (1973) Anthony Quinn, Frederic Forrest. 2:00 . . . . .MAX
- ❑ Nashville Now/Ricky Van Shelton; Shenandoah; Shelby Lynne. . . . . . .NASH
- ❑ Jimmy Neutron. . . . NICK
- ❑ Emeril. . . . . FOOD

- ❑ Baseball/United States vs. Taiwan. From Tulsa, Okla. (Live) . . . . FOX
- ❑ Movie/"The Barbarians" (1987) David Paul, Peter Paul. 1:30 . . . . TMC
- ❑ Movie/"They Were Expendable" (Color) (1945) Robert Montgomery, John Wayne. 2:55. . . . . .TNT
- ❑ Walker, Texas Ranger/ Walker seeks the killer of an arrogant professor with many enemies. 1:00 . . . . USA
- ❑ Cold Case 1:00 . . . WWOR

Cable Key

A&E—Arts and Entertainment	NASH—Nashville
BRAVO—Bravo Network	NESN—N.E. Sports Network
CNN—Cable News Network	FOX—Fox Sports Net
DIS—Disney	SHO—Showtime
ESPN—Entertainment/ Sports Network	TMC—Turner Movie Classics
	USA—USA Network
HBO—Home Box Office	WWOR—New York
LIFE—Lifetime	WTBS—Atlanta
MAX—Cinemax	

1. The schedule gives programs starting at
   _____7:00 p.m._____

2. How many movies are being shown at 8:00 tonight? _____

3. How many food programs are being shown at 8:00 tonight? _____

4. The program I'd like to watch at 8:00 is _____ because
   _____.

5. There are _____ sports programs starting at 7:30.

6. "HBO" means _____.

7. Three movie channels on cable are _____, _____, and _____.

8. You can watch "Rugrats" on _____ at _____

9. You can watch a program about Russian wildlife at _____.

10. The movie with Dan Aykroyd is _____

SKILL OBJECTIVE: Reading a TV schedule. Have students skim the TV schedule. Point out that it is from an area that has cable television as well as broadcast TV. Ask various students, *What show would you watch at 8:00? What channel is it on? When is the show over?* Assign the page for independent written work. As an extension, ask students to get a TV schedule for the coming week, and each day, circle the shows they watch. At the end of the week, have students graph the number of hours they watched TV each day. Bar or line graphs can be used.

Marvelous Microwaves

Language Objectives
Answer questions about a reading. Write an essay that explains how an appliance works.

Read the article.

Microwave ovens are everywhere. People use them in their homes, schools, hospitals, restaurants, and office buildings. Using one is a snap. Put a plate of food in the oven. Set the time and the temperature and ZAP! The food is hot almost instantly. It's one of those inventions that people take for granted and can't live without.

Have you ever wondered how a microwave oven works? The science behind it sounds more like science fiction. But it's not fiction. It's fact. A microwave oven cooks with radio waves, called microwaves. These waves are similar to those that send music to your radio. But microwaves have a different frequency, about 2,500 megahertz.

Water, fats, and sugars get "excited" when microwaves pass through them. They start to move! The movement of these molecules inside the food produces heat. Microwaves can produce a lot of heat in a short period of time.

Interestingly, microwaves do not affect ceramics, glass, or plastic. So in a microwave oven, the food gets hot, but the dish stays cold.

You may be thinking, "My body has water, fats, and, sugars inside it." You are right. If the microwaves could escape the oven, your molecules would get excited, too. But microwaves bounce off metal. The oven is made of metal. The door has a metal shield to keep the microwaves from escaping.

A Now answer the questions.

1. What causes food in a microwave oven to cook?

    a. radio waves from a radio

    b. microwaves that excite molecules in food

    c. heat from the plate

2. What keeps microwaves from escaping?

    a. food   **b.** ceramic, glass, and plastic   **c.** metal

3. Write the numbers 1–3 to show the sequence in which things happen when you cook food in a microwave oven.

    _____ The food gets hot.

    _____ Microwaves pass through the food.

    _____ Molecules in the food get "excited."

B Conventional ovens work very differently from a microwave oven. Find out how an electric or gas stove works. Write a short essay about it in your notebook.

SKILL OBJECTIVES: Determining cause and effect; sequencing. Have students read the article silently. Tell them to look at the diagram as they read the selection. They may want to reread one or more times to be sure they understand how the microwave works. *Part A:* Tell students they are going to scan, or look quickly through the article to find specific information that will help them answer the questions. *Part B:* Students can find information about stoves heated by gas or electricity in books, an encyclopedia, or the Internet. The school librarian can help them locate this information.

Dear Dot

Dear Dot,
    We are going to have to move soon, and my husband and I are having trouble deciding where to go. I want to stay in the city. Fred wants to buy a house way out in the suburbs. He works at home, so he isn't going to have to commute. But I am going to have to drive 35 miles to work every day. I am going to have to get up earlier, and arrive home later each evening. Besides, I love the city and I hate to drive! Dot, we don't know what to do. How can we compromise?

                                            City Lover

1. What are City Lover and her husband going to have to do soon? _____

_____

2. What does her husband want to do? _____

_____

3. Why does City Lover not want to do what her husband wants? _____

_____

4. What does the word *commute* in this letter mean? Circle your answer.

   a. speak with someone

   b. add up

   c. arrange something

   d. travel to and from a place

5. What is your advice to City Lover? Discuss your answer in class. Then write a letter to her telling her what you think she should do.

   Dear City Lover,

   _____

   _____

   _____

   _____

   _____

   _____

   _____

SKILL OBJECTIVES: Reading for details; drawing conclusions; making judgments; writing a letter. Have students read the letter and answer questions 1–4 independently. Correct these as a class. Then have students discuss question 5 and write their letters. Have several volunteers read their letters and have the class make suggestions for rephrasing, etc. As an additional option, ask students to write a paragraph about where they would like to live (city, country, suburbs), listing the advantages of the area they choose.

53

A As you read the story to yourself, change the verbs in parentheses to the past tense. Then write the whole story with the past tense verbs in your notebook. The first two sentences are done for you.

I (get) on the bus. I (sit) next to a lady that I (know). She (asks) me a million questions. Where (do) I go to school? Who (are) my friends? What (is) my favorite class? Then she (asks) who (is) my favorite teacher. So I (tell) her a story.

I (come) from Mexico. In second grade, I (move) to America. I (don't) speak English. On the first day of school, my teacher (says) something. I (don't) understand a word she (says). She (points) to the back of the class. I (see) a door. I (think) she (wants) me to go there. So I (walk) to the back of the class and into the closet. The kids (laugh) at me. I (feel) so embarrassed. I (want) to run away. My teacher (leads) me to my seat. She was pointing to the seat, not to the closet.

Then my teacher (says) something and the kids (line) up. I (am) scared. What (are) they going to do? My teacher (shakes) my hand. She (points) to herself and (says), "I am Mrs. Valdez." She (points) to me and (says), "I am Pilar." Then she (says) in Spanish, "Repitame." I (repeat) what she (says). I (say), "I am Pilar." Mrs. Valdez (smiles). One by one the kids in class (shake) my hand and (say) their names. I (say), "I am Pilar" to each one. I (don't) feel embarrassed anymore. I spoke English!

The lady that I (know) (says) my favorite teacher (is) a gem. I (know) she was right.

I got on the bus. I sat next to a lady I knew.

B Read each of the sentences below. Write _T_ if the sentence is true. Write _F_ if it is false. Write _?_ if the story doesn't give you enough information to decide.

1. Pilar sat next to a man on the bus. _____

2. Pilar was from Mexico. _____

3. Pilar hated school. _____

4. Pilar did not speak English her first day of school. _____

5. Pilar thought the teacher told her to go into the closet. _____

6. The kids in class called her nasty names. _____

7. Pilar felt embarrassed. _____

8. Mrs. Valdez is Pilar's favorite teacher. _____

9. Mrs. Valdez is Mexican. _____

C In your notebook, write about an embarrassing experience you have had. Tell what happened. Tell when and where it happened. Describe how you felt about it.

People and Places

Language Objectives
Name a person or place by using context clues. Write complex sentences using <u>who</u> or <u>where</u> as a conjunction.

A Read each sentence. Use the Data Bank to find the person it describes. The first one is done for you.

1. He's a person who helps you plan a vacation or trip. _____travel agent_____

2. She's a person who writes books, plays, or stories. _____

3. He's a person who cuts meat at the supermarket. _____

4. She's a person who fills cavities and pulls teeth. _____

5. He's a person who stays with young children when their parents go out for the evening. _____

6. She's a person who gives you information when you dial 411 or 1-555-1212. _____

7. He's a person who decides if a baseball player is out or is safe. _____

8. She's a person who leads a chorus or an orchestra. _____

B Use the Data Bank to find the place each sentence describes. The first one is done for you.

1. It's a place where there is lots of sand and very little rain. _____desert_____

2. It's a place where people play basketball. _____

3. It's a place where you go to wash your clothes. _____

4. It's a place where you go when you want to shop in many different kinds of stores. _____

5. It's a place where you go to see clowns, animals, and acrobats. _____

6. It's a place where you go to see famous paintings and drawings. _____

7. It's a place where you go to buy a watch or a necklace. _____

8. It's a place where you go to buy a sofa or a bed. _____

DATA BANK

author	babysitter	butcher	circus	conductor	court
dentist	~~desert~~	furniture store	jewelry store	laundromat	mall
museum	operator	~~travel agent~~	umpire		

C Finish these sentences. Use *who* or *where* in each sentence. The first one is done for you.

1. An astronaut _____is a person who travels in space._____

2. A lawyer _____

3. A stadium _____

4. A zoo _____

5. An architect _____

SKILL OBJECTIVES: Using adjective clauses with *who* and *where*; discussing occupations and community places; drawing conclusions. Have students complete Parts A and B independently. Draw attention to the phrases *a person who* and *a place where*. Have students complete Part C. Ask volunteers to read their favorite sentence aloud. *Extension Activity:* Some students may enjoy creating crossword puzzles with occupation and community places vocabulary. Check the puzzles for accuracy, then reproduce and distribute to the class to solve.

A Nation of Immigrants (1)

Language Objectives
Answer questions about a reading. Support an opinion by writing an expository paragraph.

A Look at the graph. It shows the number of people who immigrated (came into) the United States between 1901 and 1998. It also shows where these people came from. Use the graph to complete the sentences. The first one is done for you.

Regional Origins of Immigrants to the United States

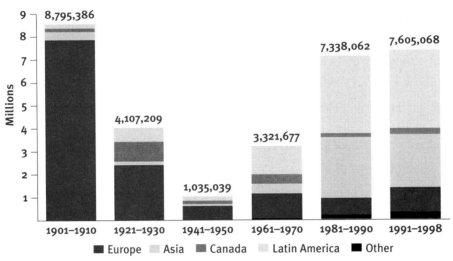

Source: INS Statistical Yearbook

1. About ___8.8___ million people came to the United States between 1901 and 1910.

2. Most of the people who first came between 1901 and 1930 were from _____.

3. Most of those who came between 1981 and 1998 were from _____.

4. People from Europe were the largest number of immigrants from _____ to _____.

5. Many people from Asia came to the United States after the year _____.

6. About _____ million immigrants came to the United States between 1901 and 1910.

7. About _____ million immigrants came to the United States between 1981 and 1998.

8. In which period did the most immigrants come to the United States? _____

9. Not many immigrants came between 1941 and 1950 probably because _____

_____ (Hint: look at page 6.)

10. Which region has had the least number of immigrants overall? _____

B The United States has been called "a nation of immigrants." In your notebook, write a paragraph telling why this is or is not a good name. Are there any people in the United States who are not immigrants or descendants of immigrants? Discuss your answer with others in the class.

SKILL OBJECTIVES: Interpreting graphs; writing a paragraph. Read the introductory paragraph, then draw attention to the graph. Ask, *Where have most U.S. immigrants come from? Where did your family come from? How many U.S. immigrants have come from that part of the world? How many immigrants came from ... between (1901 and 1910)? Between (1961 and 1970), where did most immigrants come from?* Assign the page for independent written work.

A Nation of Immigrants (2)

Language Objective
Answer questions about a reading.

On the preceding page is a graph showing the history of immigration into the United States. On this page is a table dealing with immigration from seven countries for the years 1981 to 2001. Look at the table. Then do Parts A and B below.

Where Immigrants Were Born

Place	Number
Italy	58,600
China	869,800
Japan	114,300
Thailand	117,100
Nigeria	110,900
Haiti	349,100
Brazil	85,500

Source: Statistical Abstract of the United States

A **Answer these questions.**

1. Which country had the greatest number of people who came to live in the United States between 1981 and 2001? _____

2. Which country had the least number of people who came to live in the United States between 1981 and 2001? _____

3. Which two countries on the table had fewer than 100,000 people come to live in the United States between 1981 and 2001? _____

4. Which countries had more than 100,000 people who came to the United States to live between 1981 and 2001? _____

B **Read each of the following statements. Use the table to decide whether it is true or false. Write _T_ if it is true. Write _F_ if it is false. Write _?_ if the material doesn't give you enough information to decide.**

1. Most of the people who came to the United States between 1981 and 2001 were from Africa. _____

2. Between 1981 and 2001, the number of Italians who came was about half the number of Nigerians. _____

3. More people came from Brazil than from Italy. _____

4. About 500,000 Haitians came to the United States during this period. _____

5. The third largest group to come during this period was from Thailand. _____

6. By now the group of immigrants from China would probably be over a million. _____

7. Other groups not on the table have groups of immigrants that number a million. _____

C **In your notebook, make graphs of the information in the table.**

SKILL OBJECTIVES: Reading tables; graphing statistics. Help students locate the countries on a world map. Students can work in pairs on Parts A and B. _Part C:_ Have students draw bar graphs and label their graphs (U.S. Immigration, 1981–2001). Color and label each section. For the bar graph, number the vertical axis from 0–900,000 in steps of 30,000.

What Did You See?

Language Objective
Combine simple sentences to make complex sentences.

A Read the pairs of sentences. Make each pair of sentences into one sentence. Look at the example, and use it as a model for your answers.

Example: Yesterday I saw a man. He was sleeping in the subway station.

Yesterday I saw a man who was sleeping in the subway station.

1. Yesterday I saw a girl. She was walking six dogs at one time!

_____

_____

2. Yesterday I saw an old woman. She was looking in trash cans for food.

_____

_____

3. Yesterday I saw a man. He was wearing a clown costume and handing out flyers about the circus.

_____

_____

4. Yesterday I saw a boy. He was roller-blading down a busy street.

_____

_____

5. Yesterday I saw a girl. She was eating three ice-cream cones at the same time.

_____

_____

6. Yesterday I saw a young man on the subway. He was taking a box of kittens to the pet store.

_____

_____

B Now use the pictures to write the third line of the dialogue. The first one is done for you.

1. Do you know Rita Marini?

No, I don't. Who is she?

She's the girl who lives next door to me.

2. Do you know Kinchee Chow?

No, I don't. Who is she?

_____

_____

SCHOOL BUS

SKILL OBJECTIVE: Combining sentences with *who*. Go over the directions with the class, then assign the page as independent written work.

58

Word Skills: Prefixes

A prefix is a syllable or group of syllables that comes at the beginning of a word and has a special meaning. You can add a prefix to another word or root word to change the meaning of the original word or to create a new word. Look at the list of common prefixes below and the examples of each one.

Prefix and Meaning	Example and Definition
mono = one	monorail: train running on one rail
bi = two	bicycle: two-wheeled vehicle
tri = three	triangle: three-sided figure
poly = many	polytheism: belief in many gods
un = not	unwelcome: not welcome or wanted
pre = before	prehistoric: before recorded history
ex = out	export: send out of a country
sub = under	subterranean: under the ground
inter = between	international: between nations
re = again	reread: read again

Now match the columns. Write the letter of the correct definition in the space next to the word. Use your dictionary if you need to. The first one is done for you.

1. premature   b
2. monotone   _____
3. bilingual   _____
4. exhale   _____
5. subtitle   _____
6. interstellar   _____
7. polygon   _____
8. tripod   _____
9. unprepared   _____
10. reorder   _____
11. preface   _____
12. monopoly   _____
13. extract   _____
14. biweekly   _____
15. subway   _____
16. triple   _____
17. polygamy   _____
18. interfere   _____
19. rewrite   _____
20. uncertain   _____

a. speaks two languages
b. before the expected time
c. copy or write again
d. one company in control of an entire business
e. to remove or pull out
f. not ready
g. multiply by three
h. many-sided figure
i. translation on a foreign film
j. one constant tone of voice
k. come between
l. not sure
m. train that travels under the ground
n. breathe out
o. between the stars
p. ask for supplies again
q. every two weeks
r. three-legged support
s. introduction to a book; foreword
t. many wives for one husband

SKILL OBJECTIVE: Understanding prefixes. Go over the introduction and chart with the class. Complete the first items together. Have students identify the prefix used, recall its meaning from the chart, put it together with the root word meaning, if possible, and choose the most likely answer. Remind students to first answer the easier items, then return to the more difficult ones. *Extension Activity:* Have students use the twenty words in original sentences. They may use dictionaries to confirm and refine their understanding of the words.

59

Travel by Rail

A Make sure you know the meaning of the underlined words in the article.

transportation	locomotive	stagecoach	imagination
machine	technology	challenged	crisscrossed
steam	railroad		

B Read the article quickly to get some general ideas about it. Then read it again more slowly to answer the questions.

In Europe in the late 1700s, there was a system of transportation called a tramway. Horses pulled wagons along rails made of wood and metal. In 1803, a Welshman named Samuel Homfray had an idea for a better way to travel. What if a machine could pull the wagons instead? A machine could pull a bigger load faster than a horse. Homfray hired Richard Trevithick to make such a machine to use at his ironworks. In 1804, Mr. Trevithick made the world's first steam locomotive. This new technology was great. But the locomotive ran only three times. Each time its weight broke the rails.

A sturdier railway system with iron rails replaced the tramway. George Stevenson built the first locomotive engine for a railroad. In 1825, his train pulled 450 people and six cars full of coal. Train travel began in England and then spread to other European countries and the United States.

In the United States, an American businessman named Peter Cooper owned land near the Baltimore and Ohio Railroad. He wanted the railroad to be successful. So he designed and built his own locomotive in 1830. It was small, but powerful. Cooper called his locomotive the *Tom Thumb* after a storybook character. At that time, the stagecoach was a popular mode of transportation. A stagecoach company challenged the *Tom Thumb* to a race. Cooper accepted.

"On your mark, get set, go!" The stagecoach pulled out ahead. The *Tom Thumb* began to build up steam. Soon the engine was chugging down the track. It caught up to the horse, and then it passed the horse. The *Tom Thumb* was going to win. Suddenly, something went wrong. An engine part broke. The *Tom Thumb* rumbled to a stop and the stagecoach won. But in the end, the locomotive was the real winner. It excited the imagination and interest of the American public. The country was expanding. People wanted to head west. Improvements in transportation needed to be made to meet ever-growing demands for goods. The locomotive was the answer. By 1870, railroads crisscrossed the United States.

C Think carefully and answer the following question.

Why were locomotives better than horses for pulling wagons or trains?

a. Locomotives didn't need to eat hay.

b. Locomotives were big.

c. Locomotives could pull heavier loads faster.

d. Locomotives ran on rails.

(Go on to the next page.)

SKILL OBJECTIVES: Reading comprehension; drawing conclusions; building vocabulary. Review the directions with the students. After the first reading, you may want to lead a discussion about the meaning of the highlighted vocabulary words. Encourage students to check and refine their definitions by using a dictionary.

D **Use a word from the underlined vocabulary to complete each sentence.**

1. Flying cars may be the future of _____.
2. My iron has a setting for _____.
3. Plasma screens are the latest _____ in TV sets.
4. It takes _____ to be a good inventor.
5. My teacher _____ me to do my best.

E **Answer these questions in your notebook.**

1. What mode of transportation was in use in the late 1700s?
2. What did the horses pull?
3. In what year did Richard Trevithick invent the steam locomotive?
4. Who made the first railroad locomotive?
5. Who was Peter Cooper?

6. What was the *Tom Thumb*?
7. What kind of vehicle challenged the *Tom Thumb* to a race?
8. Which vehicle won?
9. What happened after this race?
10. How many years did it take for railroads to crisscross the United States?

F **People have always made up names for widely used inventions. Some of these names are in the column at the left. See if you can match them up with the inventions they name. Write the letter of the invention in the blank in front of its "folk" name.**

1. iron horse _____
2. flying machine _____
3. talkies _____
4. tin lizzie _____
5. idiot box _____
6. nickelodeon _____
7. bullhorn _____
8. skyscraper _____
9. flattop _____
10. whirlybird _____

a. television
b. aircraft carrier
c. electric voice amplifier
d. coin-operated phonograph
e. tall building
f. locomotive
g. movies with sound
h. helicopter
i. Model T Ford
j. airplane

G **Imagine it is 1804. People are faced with a choice. Do they stick with horses, or do they turn to the new technology of steam locomotives? Draw a chart like the one below in your notebook. Write three arguments to support each kind of transportation.**

Advantages of Horses	Advantages of Locomotives
1.	1.
2.	2.
3.	3.

SKILL OBJECTIVES: Reading for details; building vocabulary; making inferences; discussing opposing viewpoints; making a study chart. Students should complete Parts D and E independently. Parts F and G may best be done with a partner.

Dear Dot

Language Objectives
Answer questions about a reading. Give advice. Agree or disagree with advice.

Dear Dot,
   My friend Larry asked me to lend him one of my CDs last week. I am very careful with my CDs, and I don't usually let people borrow them, but Larry is my best friend, so I let him take it. He returned it yesterday, and it's ruined! There are big scratches on it. When I bought this CD last year, it cost me $15.00. Now it's even more expensive. I think Larry owes me a new CD. What do you think?

                                        Bob

1. What did Larry ask Bob last week? _____

_____

2. Why did Bob agree to do this? _____

_____

3. What is the condition of Bob's CD now? _____

_____

4. What does Bob want? _____

5. What does the word *lend* in this letter mean? Circle the best answer.

   a. give for a while

   b. take for a while

   c. spend

   d. break or ruin

6. What do you think Bob should do? Discuss your answer in class. Then write your advice in a letter to Bob. How can he get what he wants without losing a friend?

   Dear Bob, _____

_____

_____

_____

_____

_____

_____

_____

                                        _____

SKILL OBJECTIVES: Reading for details; drawing conclusions; making judgments; writing a letter. Have students read the letter and answer questions 1–5 independently. Correct these as a class. Then have students discuss question 6 and write their letters. Have several volunteers read their letters and have the class make suggestions for rephrasing, etc. As an additional option, have students write about a hobby or other interest, explaining what the hobby or interest is and how, where, and when they first found out about it.

A Trip to the Moon: 1865

Language Objective
Complete a reading using context clues.

Use words from the Data Bank to fill the blanks in the article. Write only one word in each blank. The same word can be used more than once, however. The first one is done for you.

Jules Verne is a famous French author who dreamed about wonderful machines and fantastic journeys. In 1865 Verne wrote _____*a*_____ book about a trip to _____ moon. The name of the _____ was *From the Earth to the Moon*. The spaceship he described _____ very interesting. There were three "astronauts" in the spaceship—two Americans and _____ Frenchman. The _____ kept chickens in the ship for food! _____ beds they used were very comfortable, _____ they cooked their meals on _____ gas stove!

The men reached the _____ in 97 hours 13 minutes _____ 20 seconds after _____ had left the Earth. When they landed on the _____, they made a mistake and couldn't leave _____ spaceship. That was a good thing _____ they didn't have any spacesuits!

Verne's books were very popular. _____ at that time _____ fascinated with scientific developments and Verne included many scientific facts. Today we call _____ like this "science fiction."

In 1865 _____ thought Verne's dreams _____ impossible. But 104 years later, _____ were walking on the moon.

DATA BANK						
~~a~~	and	because	book	books	men	moon
one	people	the	they	was	were	

SKILL OBJECTIVE: Completing a cloze exercise. Assign this page for independent written work. Correct as a class and ask comprehension questions about the article. *Extension Activities:* Have students check the school library for books by or about Jules Verne. Other students can use an encyclopedia or the Internet to research Jules Verne. Have students report their findings to the class.

A Trip to the Moon: 1969

Read the article. Use your dictionary for any words you are not sure of.

In the early 1960s, the United States challenged itself to land people on the moon before the end of the decade. But, space travel was in its infancy. It had been only a few short years since manned spacecraft could orbit the Earth. A moon landing would be more complicated and dangerous. Could it be done? Scientists went to work to prove it could.

First, unmanned missions were sent more than 238,000 miles to the moon to see what the moon was like. Different crafts took thousands of pictures of the moon and tested the air and soil. Then manned flights were sent to the moon to see if people could get there and return safely. Finally, a spacecraft that could land astronauts on the moon and return to Earth was readied. It was called *Apollo 11*.

The ship had three main parts. There was a life-support section called the service module. This provided air, water, and electricity for the astronauts. It had a command module called *Columbia*, where the astronauts lived and worked. Then there was a landing module (LM) that would land on the moon. This was called *Eagle*.

On July 16, 1969, *Apollo 11* was ready to go. The spacecraft mounted on a massive rocket was launched from the Kennedy Space Center in Florida. On board were three astronauts: Michael Collins, Edwin Aldrin, and Neil Armstrong.

It took four days for the astronauts to get to the moon. When they reached the Sea of Tranquility, *Eagle* separated from *Columbia*. Edwin Aldrin and Neil Armstrong piloted the LM down to the moon. The world held its breath until it heard Aldrin say, "The Eagle has

landed." Then people watched in amazement as Neil Armstrong opened the hatch and stepped to the surface. He said, "That's one small step for a man, one giant leap for mankind." The scientists had done it! On July 20, 1969, the United States had put people on the moon with five months to spare!

Read each sentence below and decide if it is true or false. Write *T* if it is true. Write *F* if it is false. Write *?* if the story doesn't give you enough information to decide.

1. Traveling to space was common before 1960. _____

2. The moon is about 238,000 miles from the Earth. _____

3. *Apollo 11* had five main parts. _____

4. The command module *Columbia* landed on the moon. _____

5. *Apollo 11* was launched on July 20, 1969. _____

6. It took the astronauts four days to reach the moon. _____

7. Six other *Apollo* LMs landed on the moon. _____

8. Neil Armstrong was the first person to walk on the moon. _____

SKILL OBJECTIVES: Reading for details; reviewing verb tenses. Have students read the selection quickly to get a general idea of the subject. List and discuss unfamiliar vocabulary. Students should use context clues and try to guess the meaning. Have students read the article again and answer the questions. *Extension Activities:* Ask students to: 1) name the main idea of the story, 2) find diagrams and photos of *Apollo 11* and the lunar voyage in the library, 3) list three things people might be able to do 100 years from now.

Space Exploration

The words *already* and *yet* are often used with the present perfect tense. Look at the box to see how they are used. The box also has a review of the present perfect and past tenses.

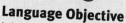

Language Objective
Write answers and questions using the present perfect tense and the adverbs <u>yet</u> or <u>already</u>.

already:	Astronauts have already been to the moon.	(affirmative)
yet:	Astronauts haven't been to Mars yet.	(negative)
	Have astronauts been to Mars yet?	(question)
Non-specific time:	A woman has already traveled into space.	(present perfect)
Specific time:	In 1963, Valentina Tereshkova was the first woman to travel into space.	(past)

Use *already* and *yet* in the following sentences. The first two are done for you.

1. Unmanned spacecraft (land) on Mars. (affirmative)

   Unmanned spacecraft have already landed on Mars.

2. People (travel) to the planet Mars. (negative)

   People haven't traveled to the planet Mars yet.

3. The Hubble telescope (send) thousands of images to Earth. (affirmative)

   _____

4. The Hubble telescope (photograph) new galaxies. (affirmative)

   _____

5. Women (travel) in outer space. (question)

   _____

6. The spaceship *Voyager* (fly) beyond our solar system. (affirmative)

   _____

7. We (discover) any new planets. (negative)

   _____

8. Scientists (find) ten new moons around Uranus. (affirmative)

   _____

9. Spacecraft (go) to Venus. (question).

   _____

10. Other countries (be) to the moon. (negative)

    _____

DATA BANK

past participles

| sent | traveled | landed | photographed | been | found | discovered | flown | gone |

SKILL OBJECTIVE: Using the present perfect with *already* and *yet*. Review the construction of the present perfect tense and remind students of the difference between non-specific and specific time, as shown in the box at the top of the page. Provide other examples on the board, if necessary. If students need more practice than the two items already done for them, go through the entire page orally before assigning it for independent written work.

Present Perfect *vs.* Past

The present perfect tells about something that happened at an unspecified time (or times) in the past.

> I *have been* to New York three times.
>
> He *has* already *visited* the Museum of Science.

The past tense tells about something that happened at a specific time (or times) in the past.

> I *was* in New York three years ago.
>
> He *visited* the Museum of Science last month.

A Read the sentences carefully and choose either the present perfect or the past form of the verb. The first one is done for you.

1. Astronauts (travel) ___*have traveled*___ to the moon several times.

2. The first one (walk) _____ on the moon in 1969. Two years later, two Americans (return) _____ and (drive) _____ a Moon Rover. The top speed of the "car" (be) _____ 7 miles an hour.

3. Although astronauts (be) _____ in outer space may times, they (not/land) _____ on any planets yet.

4. The first woman cosmonaut, Valentina Tereshkova, (spend) _____ seventy hours in space in 1963.

5. The United States (launch) _____ its first satellite in 1958 and since then we (send) _____ many different kinds of satellites into space.

6. In 1987 a Russian cosmonaut (live) _____ in a space station for 326 days. Imagine living in space for nearly a year!

7. Yuri Gagarin (be) _____ the first person in space, and Neil Armstrong and Buzz Aldrin (be) _____ the first to land on the moon.

B Write a question to go with each answer. Use the present perfect or past tense.

1. ___*Who was the first person in space?*___
   (Yuri Gagarin was.)

2. _____?
   (She spent seventy hours in space.)

3. _____?
   (Yes, they have.)

4. _____?
   (In 1969.)

5. _____?
   (Armstrong and Aldrin were.)

6. _____?
   (For 362 days.)

SKILL OBJECTIVES: Contrasting present perfect and past tenses; asking questions. Call attention to the grammar explanation at the top of the page. If students need more examples, provide them on the board. If students are still unsure about when to use the present perfect and when to use the past tense, go through all of Part A orally before assigning it for written work. *Part B*: Do the first two items as a class before assigning it for independent written work.

Word Skills: Irregular Plurals

Some plurals are difficult to form because of irregular spellings or because there are special rules for them. Look at the following rules for forming plurals. But be careful! There are many exceptions to these rules. Get into the habit of using your dictionary to check your work. It will give you the information you need about spelling irregularities and exceptions to the rules.

Rule 1:	For words that end in a consonant followed by *y*, change the *y* to *i* and add *-es* to form the plural. Example: party → parties
Rule 2:	For words that end in *sh, ch, x,* and s, add *-es* to form the plural. Examples: brush → brushes church → churches tax → taxes kiss → kisses
Rule 3:	For words that end in *f* or *fe*, change the *f* or *fe* to *v* and add *-es*. Examples: shelf → shelves life → lives There are many exceptions to this rule.
Rule 4:	Compound nouns form their plural by adding *-s* to the most important word in the phrase. Example: mother-in-law → mothers-in-law
Rule 5:	For words that end in a consonant followed by *o*, add *-es* to form the plural. Example: potato → potatoes There are many exceptions to this rule, so check your dictionary.
Rule 6:	Some words have special plural forms and do not take an *-s* at all. Example: man → men
Rule 7:	Some words (mostly animal names) keep the same form in singular and plural. Example: deer → deer

Make the following words plural. Use your dictionary.

1. thief _____

2. father-in-law _____

3. piano _____

4. penny _____

5. box _____

6. tooth _____

7. roof _____

8. tomato _____

9. mouse _____

10. scarf _____

11. moose _____

12. monkey _____

13. wife _____

14. foot _____

15. silo _____

16. wolf _____

17. sheep _____

18. chief _____

19. half _____

20. woman _____

21. pony _____

22. boss _____

23. wish _____

24. watch _____

SKILL OBJECTIVES: Constructing irregular plurals; using the dictionary to check spelling. Review the rules with class, then assign the page for independent written work. Have students correct their own work by using a dictionary.

Fourth Rock from the Sun

Language Objectives
Define vocabulary. Answer questions about a reading. Determine the correct sequence of statements from a reading.

A Make sure you know the meaning of the following important words underlined in the article.

reality	mission	orbit	lander	rover
spacecraft	launched	Martian	orbiter	lab

B Read the article quickly to get some general ideas about it. Then read it again more slowly to answer the questions.

Mars

A hundred years ago, people only dreamed about traveling to the moon. But in 1969, that dream became <u>reality</u>. Two astronauts, Neil Armstrong and Edwin Aldrin, walked on the moon, while Michael Collins stayed in the <u>spacecraft</u>. Today, we only dream about traveling to Mars. But one day, this dream might become a reality, too.

Scientists have been exploring the red planet from Earth and from unmanned spacecraft. They are finding out as much as they can about the fourth rock from the sun.

The first <u>mission</u> to Mars was just a fly-by. The *Mariner 4* was <u>launched</u> on November 5, 1965. It flew past Mars eight months later on July 14, 1965. It gave scientists their first good look at the planet. But the *Mariner 4* just kept going and couldn't stop to explore more.

The next step was to send a spacecraft that could <u>orbit</u> Mars. This way the scientist could get a much better look and start making maps of the planet. The *Mariner 9* craft was launched on May 30, 1971. *Mariner 9* orbited Mars for over a year. In that time, it mapped 100% of the surface of the planet. It found dry riverbeds, a canyon 3,000 miles long, and the largest volcano in the solar system. *Mariner 9* also took pictures of the two <u>Martian</u> moons, Phobos and Deimos.

The next challenge was to land on Mars. The *Viking 1* was launched on August 20, 1975 and landed on July 20, 1976. The spacecraft had two parts, a <u>lander</u> and an <u>orbiter</u>. The lander ran all sorts of tests on the surface. It checked the soil. It checked the weather. And it looked for signs of life. The *Viking* orbiter sent the information back to Earth and took countless pictures.

Mars Rover

The most recent Mars mission is called the Mars Exploration Rover Mission. This craft landed on Mars in January 2004. The <u>rover</u> is a science <u>lab</u> on wheels. It can move across the surface of the planet. It has a camera that takes three-dimensional pictures.

Look how far we've come in the last fifty years! We are much closer to the goal of sending people to Mars. It's not such an impossible task. It could even happen in your lifetime.

C Think carefully and answer the following question.

Why are scientists studying the planet Mars?

a. They like to make maps of Mars.

b. They want to take pictures of Mars.

c. They want to test the soil of Mars.

d. They want to find out everything there is to know about Mars.

(Go on to the next page.)

SKILL OBJECTIVES: Reading comprehension; interpreting idiomatic expressions; building vocabulary. Review the directions with the students. After the first reading, you may want to lead a discussion about the meaning of the highlighted vocabulary words. Encourage students to check and refine their definitions by using a dictionary.

D Circle the answer that best completes the sentence.

Some people's dream came true in 1969 because

a. we know everything about the moon.

b. the moon is our closest neighbor.

c. three astronauts flew to the moon.

d. Michael Collins stayed in the spacecraft.

E Use a word from the underlined vocabulary to complete each of these sentences.

a. We watched the spacecraft being _____.

b. The part of the *Viking* spacecraft that touched Mars was the _____.

c. The part of *Viking* that stayed above Mars was the _____.

d. In January 2004, a _____ to Mars landed there.

e. The word _____ is probably a short form of the word *laboratory*.

F Write the answers to these questions in your notebook.

1. How long did it take *Mariner 4* to get to Mars?

2. Why did *Mariner 4* just fly by Mars?

3. What might finding dry riverbeds on Mars suggest to scientists?

4. How many moons does Earth have?

5. Does our moon have a name?

6. How many moons does Mars have?

7. What are the Martian moons called?

8. In your opinion, when do you think people will go to Mars?

G Number these events in the order in which they happened.

_____ Armstrong and Aldrin walked on the moon.

_____ The *Mariner 9* flew around Mars.

_____ The *Mariner 4* flew past Mars.

_____ The rover landed on Mars in 2004.

_____ *Viking I* landed on Mars in 1976.

H Write a paragraph in your notebook that answers these questions. Use an encyclopedia or the Internet if you need to, but write your paragraph(s) in your own words.

a. What color is Mars?

b. Why was this planet named Mars?

c. What is another meaning for Mars?

SKILL OBJECTIVES: Reading for details; drawing inferences; sequencing; paraphrasing information from an encyclopedia or the Internet. Assign Parts C–G as independent written work. Correct and discuss as a class. Have students use the encyclopedia, a science book or the Internet to research the questions in Part H and bring their notes back for a classroom discussion. Help students organize the information they have gathered and restate the facts in their own words. Paraphrasing is a difficult skill. Present students with techniques, and provide lots of group practice.

Library Catalog Cards

Read the following text.

A library card catalog is a complete list, in card form, of the books owned by the library. To find out if the library owns a particular book, you look for that book in the catalog. To help you, the catalog has three kinds of cards for most books. There are author cards, which have the author's name at the top. There are title cards, which have the title of the book at the top. And there are subject cards, which have the subject of the book at the top. Often, all three cards are in the same set of catalog drawers. Sometimes, however, subject cards are in a separate set of drawers.

All the cards are filed alphabetically. Suppose you have a book called *Looking at the Moon*, by an author named John Adams. The author card will be filed with the A's. The title card will be filed with the L's. And the subject card will be filed with the M's (for Moon). If you look under the M's, you will find other books on the same subject written by different authors. If you look under the A's, you will find other books by the same author, perhaps on different subjects. If you look under the L's, you will find other books whose titles start with "Look" or "Looking."

All the cards give you complete information about the book, including its title, its author(s), its publisher, and its subject. They also give you information about where it is located in the library. A "call number" in the upper left-hand corner of the card identifies the section of the library where the book is kept.

Look at the list below. These are the top lines from some catalog cards. Tell which kind of card each one is. Write "author card," "title card," or "subject card" next to each one.

1. RAILROADS _____

2. E.B. White _____

3. *Huckleberry Finn* _____

4. *Moby Dick* _____

5. PILGRIMS _____

6. CIVIL WAR _____

7. Madeleine L'Engle _____

8. F. Scott Fitzgerald _____

9. *The Call of the Wild* _____

10. SLAVERY _____

11. John Steinbeck _____

12. *For Whom the Bell Tolls* _____

13. *The Groucho Letters* _____

14. NEW YORK CITY _____

15. Ellen Goodman _____

16. *A Room of One's Own* _____

17. MOVIES _____

18. THANKSGIVING _____

19. Emily Dickinson _____

20. *Pride and Prejudice* _____

```
522   Adams, John
A     Looking at the moon
      by John Adams.
```
```
522   Looking at the moon
A     by John Adams.
```
```
522   MOON
A     Looking at the moon
      by John Adams.
```

SKILL OBJECTIVE: Using the card catalog. Read and discuss the introduction together, then assign the exercises. *Extension Activities:* Have students use the card catalog to answer these questions: *1. Where are the subject cards filed in your library? 2. How many books can you find about railroads, the Pilgrims, movies, witchcraft? 3. Which books does your library have by the authors on this page? 4. Does your library have the books listed on this page? Write down the call numbers and locate the books on the shelves. 5. Does your library have its catalog on the computer? How is a computer catalog different from a card catalog?*

The Future with *Will*

One way to talk about things that are going to happen in the future is to use the verb *will*. Look at the examples below.

I will graduate.	You will leave.
He will ride.	We will arrive.
She will study.	They will stay.
It will rain.	

You can use *will* with many future expressions such as the following:

next week	next year	in a few days (weeks, months)
next month	in a year	tomorrow

A **Read the following paragraph and follow the instructions.**

We will see many changes in the world in the next twenty years, just as our parents have seen many changes in the past twenty years. Here are some of the kinds of changes some people think we will see:

1. We will drive flying cars.
2. We will find a cure for AIDS and other diseases.
3. We will all use solar energy in our homes.
4. We will be able to fly using jetpacks.
5. We will visit the moon for a vacation.

What else do you think we will do in the next twenty years? Add three changes of your own.

6. _____
   _____

7. _____
   _____

8. _____
   _____

B **Now work with a classmate asking and answering questions from the eight changes above. Use the following model:**

—Do you think we will drive flying cars in the next fifty years?

—Yes, I think we will drive flying cars. *or*

—No, I don't think we will drive flying cars.

C **Write answers to these questions in your notebook. Use complete sentences with *will*.**

1. When will you graduate from high school?
2. How old will you be on your next birthday?
3. What will you do this weekend?
4. Will you get a job or will you go to college after you graduate?
5. How old will you be when you get married?
6. When will your next school vacation begin?

SKILL OBJECTIVE: Constructing the future tense with *will*. Read the introductory paragraphs aloud. Ask students questions: *What will you do this afternoon/this weekend? When will you eat dinner tonight/have a vacation? Where will you travel someday/live ten years from now?* Assign Part A for independent written work. Have students share their favorite answer. Circulate around the room as students practice Part B. Part C may be done in class or assigned for homework.

Dear Dot

Dear Dot,

My sister Natasha keeps a diary. I know I was wrong, but one night when she left it on top of her desk I read it. Now I don't know what to do. Natasha met a boy two weeks ago, and he wants to marry her. She said no, but she wrote in her diary that every day she wants to go off with him a little bit more. You see, she's not happy at home. My parents nag her all the time because she gets bad grades in school. My problem is that if I ask my sister any questions, she will know that I read her diary. If I tell my mother, my sister will be very angry. What should I do?

Snoopy

1. Where did Natasha leave her diary? _____

_____

2. What is Natasha's secret? _____

_____

3. Why does she want to leave home? _____

_____

4. What is Snoopy's problem? _____

_____

5. What does the word *nag* mean in this letter? Circle the best answer.

  a. call and write   **b.** criticize   **c.** kiss and praise   **d.** old horse

6. What is your advice to Snoopy? Discuss your answer in class. Then play Dot's role and write a letter telling Snoopy what to do and what not to do.

_____ Dear Snoopy, _____

_____

_____

_____

_____

_____

_____

                                                    _____

SKILL OBJECTIVES: Reading for details; drawing conclusions; making judgments; writing a letter. Have students read the letter and answer questions 1–5 independently. Correct these as a class. Then have students discuss question 6 and write their letters. Ask several volunteers to read their letters and have the class make suggestions for rephrasing, etc. As an additional option, you may want to have students write a page in a diary. They should make it a fantasy that they wish would come true. The page could begin, "Dear Diary, a fantastic thing happened to me today…"

72

What Did She Tell You?

Language Objective
Use correct pronoun forms and verb structures to express reported speech.

Complete the conversations. The first one and the fourth one are done for you.

1. Please wash the dishes. — What did she tell you? — She told me to wash the dishes.

2. Please make your bed. — What did he tell you? — He _____

3. Would you mow the lawn? — What did she ask you to do? — She _____

4. Set the table. — What did he tell you to do? — He told me to set the table.

5. Would you mail this letter, please? — What did she ask you to do? — She _____

6. Do your homework! — What did they tell you? — They _____

7. Meet me in the cafeteria! — What did she want you to do? — She _____

SKILL OBJECTIVE: Reporting a speech. Write commands on pieces of paper. *Read your book. Go away. Hurry up,* etc. Write on the board, *What did he/she tell you?* Have a volunteer whisper a written command to you. The class will ask, "What did he/she tell you?" Model the answer, "She told me to ..." Have students come up in pairs. Hand a command to one student and practice these structures. Assign the page as independent written work.

The Present Perfect Progressive Tense

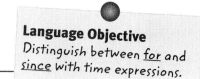

The present perfect progressive tense is used for activities that began sometime in the past and continue up to the present. Time expressions with *for* and *since* usually use this tense. Look at these examples of the present perfect progressive.

| I
You
We
They } | have been living here | { for two years.
since 1987. | He
She
It } | has been living here | { for many years.
since May. |

The example below compares the present perfect progressive with the past and present.

Past:	I started to study English two months ago.
Present:	I am studying English now.
Present perfect progressive:	I have been studying English for two months.

A **The two boxes tell you when to use *for* and when to use *since*. Read them, then complete the sentences below using *for* or *since*.**

Use *for* with general time words that describe a period or length of time, but don't give an exact date or time when and action started. For example: I have been living here ... *for* a few years. *for* a month. *for* a couple of weeks. *for* three days.	Use *since* with specific time words that tell when an action started, or with phrases that also tell when an action started. For example: I have been living here ... *since* 1975. *since* February. *since* March 19th. *since* I was a young girl.

1. Susan has been working at the bank _____ five years.
2. I have been waiting for you _____ 3:30.
3. José has been talking on the phone _____ two hours.
4. Mr. and Mrs. Chang have been living in Baltimore _____ 1986.
5. It has been raining _____ last night.
6. Mr. Steinberg has been teaching _____ he graduated from college.
7. You have been studying English _____ a long time.
8. Europeans have been coming to the Americas _____ the fifteenth century.
9. Trang has been driving _____ she was 16 years old.
10. The telephone has been ringing _____ two minutes.
11. We have been sitting in this class _____ an hour.
12. I have been thinking about you _____ a long time.
13. Pablo has been working on my portrait _____ last July.
14. That castle has been standing _____ several centuries.
15. The wreath has been on the door _____ December.
16. It has been raining _____ almost a month.

(Go on to the next page.)

B Write the sentences in the present perfect progressive form.
The first one is done for you.

1. Americans started wearing nylon clothing in 1938.

Americans have been wearing nylon clothing since 1938.

2. Astronauts started traveling in outer space in 1961.

_____

3. People started using computers in 1959.

_____

4. Americans started flying in airplanes in 1903.

_____

5. In-line skates started getting popular in the 1990s.

_____

6. Students started studying at Harvard University in 1636.

_____

C Read about Luis, and answer the questions using the correct tense.

May, 2002	came to the United States from Guatemala
June, 2002	started English classes
July, 2002	started working at a gas station
March, 2003	met Amelia
May, 2003	completed English classes
June, 2003	quit his job at gas station
July, 2003	started job at a bank
March, 2004	married Amelia

1. How long has Luis been living in the United States?

_____

2. How long did he study English?

_____

3. How long did he work at the gas station?

_____

4. When did he meet Amelia?

_____

5. How long has he been working at the bank?

_____

6. How long have Luis and Amelia been married?

_____

7. How long has Luis known Amelia?

_____

Answering Questions Correctly

Language Objective
Answer questions using correct verb tenses as prompted by question cues.

Pay attention to the question words in a sentence in order to answer them in the correct tense. Look at the following examples.

Affirmative (Yes)	
Does she live in Texas?	Yes, she lives in Texas.
Is she living in Texas?	Yes, she's living in Texas.
Did she live in Texas?	Yes, she lived in Texas.
Was she living in Texas?	Yes, she was living in Texas.
Will she live in Texas?	Yes, she will live in Texas.
Has she been living in Texas?	Yes, she has been living in Texas.
Negative (No)	
Do they work in Ohio?	No, they don't work in Ohio.
Are they working in Ohio?	No, they aren't working in Ohio.
Did they work in Ohio?	No, they didn't work in Ohio.
Were they working in Ohio?	No, they weren't working in Ohio.
Will they work in Ohio?	No, they won't work in Ohio.
Have they been working in Ohio?	No, they haven't been working in Ohio.
Other	
What school do you go to?	I go to Adams School.
What school are you going to now?	I'm going to Adams School now.
What school did you go to?	I went to Adams School.
What school were you going to then?	I was going to Adams School then.
What school will you go to?	I will go to Adams School.
What school have you been going to?	I have been going to Adams School.

Make up answers to the following questions and write them in your notebook. Make sure you use the same tense in both the question and the answer.

1. Have you been listening to the radio for a long time?
2. Where did Mark find his shoe?
3. When are you leaving?
4. What has the dog been doing all day?
5. Will your brother enjoy this book?
6. Do you eat liver?
7. Are you living in Arizona now?
8. When did you meet the Wilsons?
9. When will you decide about going on vacation?
10. How many people were living in that apartment?
11. Does this restaurant serve pizza?
12. Have you been paying your bills this year?
13. Were they driving all day yesterday?
14. Do you have a lot of money in the bank?
15. Did the glass fall on the floor?
16. Were you making a lot of money when you worked in Chicago?
17. Will you call the theater to find out when the play starts?
18. How long have you been keeping this secret for?
19. When did you take your friend to the hospital?
20. Will they apply to college in January?

SKILL OBJECTIVE: Reviewing present, past, future, and present perfect progressive tenses. Be sure students understand the differences between the tenses. A rapid-fire oral drill requiring students to use short answers *(Yes, I did/No, she wasn't)* can be fun, especially if you write or ask questions appropriate to your students. After doing the first two items together, assign the page as independent written work.

How Long and How Many?

Language Objective
Distinguish between present perfect and present perfect continuous tense.

Use complete sentences to answer the questions. The first one is done for you.

1.

2004
200,000 miles

Fran is a truck driver. She started driving a truck last year and she is driving a truck today.

How long has she been *driving* a truck? __She has been__ __driving a truck for one year.__ (time)

How many miles has she *driven* in the past year? __She has__ __driven 200,000 miles in the past year.__ (quantity)

2.

1997
3 books

Lisa is a writer. She started writing books in 1997, and she is writing today.

How long has she been *writing* books? _____

_____

How many books has she *written* since 1997? _____

_____

3.

1989
1600 students

Henry and Roberta are teachers. They both started teaching in 1989 and they are teaching today.

How long have they been *teaching*? _____

_____

How many students have they *taught* since 1989?

_____

4.

1990
401 homes

We are real estate salesmen. We started selling houses in 1990. We are selling houses today.

How long have we been *selling* houses? _____

_____

How many houses have we *sold* since 1990?

_____

5.

1961
3000 pairs

I am a shoemaker. I started making shoes in 1961. I am making shoes today.

How long have I been *making* shoes? _____

_____

How many pairs of shoes have I *made* since 1961?

_____

SKILL OBJECTIVE: Comparing present perfect progressive and present perfect. Read the first example with the class. Have a volunteer explain why the present perfect continuous is used in the first question and the present perfect in the second question. Assign the page as independent written work. *Extension Activity:* Have students draw portraits and write similar "stories" and questions about other professionals (a surgeon, two cooks, an explorer, etc.) Their classmates can read the stories and answer the questions.

An Important Science

A Make sure you know the meaning of the following important words which are underlined in the article.

complicated	molecules	escaped	examine	rusty
principles	attract	split	substances	sour
matter	collection	atoms	combine	

B Read the article quickly to get some general ideas about it. Then read it again more slowly to answer the questions.

Chemistry

Many students feel that chemistry is a difficult subject. They are so afraid of the challenge of chemistry that they don't take the time to learn anything about it. It is true that chemistry is a complicated subject, but there are some ideas and principles of chemistry that everyone can and should understand. They are:

1. All matter (all things) is made up of small separate particles called molecules.
2. Molecules move very fast and they are always moving.
3. Molecules attract each other.

Let's look at an example of these three rules. A bottle of ammonia is a collection of ammonia molecules. If you open a bottle of ammonia in a closed room, the smell is everywhere in the room. Why? Some molecules of ammonia (remember molecules are very small and you can't see them) have escaped from the bottle and are flying through the air. They cause the smell.

Why don't all of the molecules fly out of the bottle? Remember rule number three. Molecules attract each other. Most of the molecules don't escape because they are attracted to, or pulled toward, each other.

Molecules are not the smallest particles of matter. Scientists can split the molecule into smaller particles called atoms. Chemistry is the study of molecules and atoms. Chemists examine different substances and find out about their molecules and atoms. Chemists combine molecules of one substance with molecules of another. They want to see what changes take place.

Why does a nail, left outside, get rusty? Why does bread rise when you bake it? Why does milk get sour? These are all chemical changes. If you want to know what causes these chemical changes, why not try a chemistry course? Chemistry is complicated but it is also rewarding. It explains many of the occurrences of day-to-day living.

C Think carefully and answer the following question.

The rules and principles of chemistry try to explain

a. why ammonia smells.

b. why atoms are smaller than molecules.

c. the behavior and makeup of matter.

d. how fast molecules move.

(Go on to the next page.)

SKILL OBJECTIVES: Reading comprehension; identifying main idea; building vocabulary. Review the directions with the students. After the first reading, you may want to lead a discussion about the meaning of the highlighted vocabulary words. Encourage students to check and refine their definitions by using a dictionary.

D Circle the answer that best completes the sentence.

According to the principles mentioned in this article, a sliced onion makes you cry because

a. the knife splits the atoms.

b. the molecules attract each other.

c. some molecules escape and reach the eyes.

d. the molecules move very fast.

E Use a word from the underlined vocabulary to complete each of these sentences.

1. Ramon has an interesting _____ of butterflies.

2. I can't understand these directions; they're too _____.

3. The milk doesn't taste good; I think it's _____.

4. Two prisoners _____ from jail last week.

5. Artists _____ colors to make new and different shades.

F Write the answers to these questions in your notebook.

1. Why are many students afraid of chemistry?

2. What is the smallest particle of matter mentioned in the story?

3. What do chemists do?

4. Why do chemists combine molecules of different substances?

5. Why is chemistry rewarding?

G Certain things cause certain other things to happen. Look at the causes at the left. Find the effect at the right that goes with each cause, and write its letter in the blank for that cause. Use your dictionary for words you don't know.

1. too many automobiles in a city _____ **a.** damage and destruction

2. drinking too much alcohol _____ **b.** sourness

3. vitamin deficiency _____ **c.** temporary pain relief

4. tornado _____ **d.** drunkenness

5. taking aspirin tablets _____ **e.** sickness and body malfunction

6. leaving a nail outdoors _____ **f.** air pollution

7. leaving milk out of the refrigerator _____ **g.** rust

H Find out what the word *synthetic* means. What does this have to do with chemistry? Use an encyclopedia to find out some of the common things around you that have been developed by chemists. Take notes, then write a paragraph in your notebook telling the facts you have learned in your own words.

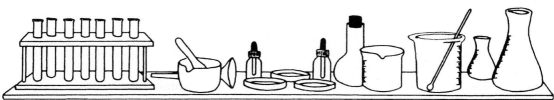

SKILL OBJECTIVES: Reading for details; drawing conclusions; understanding cause and effect; researching; writing a report.
Assign Parts C–G as independent written work. Discuss the assignment in Part H. Ask students where they will look to find the meaning of *synthetic*. What entry will they look up in the encyclopedia (chemists, chemistry, synthetics)? Will they need to read the entire article? Remind students to use the headings to skim the article until they come to the section that contains the specific information they are looking for.

Paul Pantella

Read the story.

Language Objectives
Ask questions for specific answers using correct verb tenses. Create true or false statements about a reading.

Last month, 21-year-old Paul Pantella won $100,000 in the lottery. Many young men his age might buy a sports car or a motorcycle with that kind of cash. But Paul has other plans. Paul was born in the United States. His parents came from Italy. It has been his dream to go to Italy since he was a little boy. Now his dream can come true.

Paul is planning to study in Florence, Italy, for the next two years. He loves art and architecture. What better place to study both than in the city where the Renaissance began and flourished? Many of his favorite artists lived or worked in Florence. Paul has always wanted to see Michelangelo's famous statue of David. He's anxious to see the well-known paintings by Botticelli in the Uffizzi Gallery. Paul also wants to improve his Italian. He plans to take at least one Italian class each semester. He hopes that by the end of his stay, he'll be speaking like someone born in Italy.

Paul plans to bring his parents back to their native land for his graduation.

A **Write questions about the story to fit the answers at the right. The first one is done for you. Write the last one yourself.**

1. How much ___did Paul Pantella win?___ He won $100,000.

2. How _____? He could spend the money on a sports car.

3. Where _____? He was born in the United States.

4. Where _____? His parents are from Italy.

5. Has _____? Yes, it has.

6. What _____? He plans to study art and architecture.

7. How _____? He will be there for two years.

8. Which _____? He will be in the city of Florence.

9. What _____? He has always wanted to see the statue of David.

10. Where _____? They are in the Uffizzi Gallery.

11. What _____? He wants to improve his Italian.

12. How _____? He will take one class a semester.

13. What _____? He hopes he will speak Italian well.

14. _____? _____

B **Write five true or false statements about the story in your notebook.**

For example: Paul Pantella won $10,000. (False) He is going to study in Florence. (True)

SKILL OBJECTIVES: Reviewing present perfect progressive and present perfect; simple past; *plans to/wants to*; constructing questions. Have students read the story silently, then discuss and construct the first few questions as a class. Remind students to pay close attention to the verb tense used in the answer. Assign the page as independent written work.

Word Skills: Category Labels

Look at each list of words below. Decide how the words on the list are the same, and think of a word or phrase that names or labels the list. Write the word or phrase in the blank. Use your dictionary or other books if you need to. The first list is labeled for you.

1. _____languages_____ Spanish, Chinese, Italian, Vietnamese, English

2. _____ Monopoly, chess, checkers, dominoes, Scrabble

3. _____ piano, guitar, drums, saxophone, string bass

4. _____ lily, petunia, rose, daisy, daffodil

5. _____ sofa, chair, table, bed, dresser

6. _____ wash clothes, iron, do dishes, empty trash, sweep

7. _____ Christmas, New Year, Independence Day, Thanksgiving

8. _____ poodle, collie, dalmation, German shepherd, spaniel

9. _____ penny, nickel, dime, quarter, half-dollar

10. _____ novel, dictionary, encyclopedia, Bible, atlas

11. _____ Saturn, Neptune, Pluto, Mars, Mercury

12. _____ dog, cat, fish, bird, hamster

13. _____ sparrow, robin, blue jay, eagle, pigeon

14. _____ Carson City, Austin, Sacramento, Albany, Helena

15. _____ trout, salmon, cod, shark, mackerel

16. _____ ant, grasshopper, fly, bee, cockroach

17. _____ North and South America, Europe, Africa, Asia, Australia, Antarctica

18. _____ Capricorn, Leo, Aries, Pisces, Libra

19. _____ Mary, Ruth, Tanya, Lisa, Rita

20. _____ bacon, lettuce, and tomato; ham and cheese; tuna fish; peanut butter and jelly; grilled cheese

SKILL OBJECTIVE: Classifying. Assign this page for independent written work. Correct and discuss as a class.

She and Him and They and Them

Language Objectives
Use correct pronoun forms and verb structures to express reported speech. User correct pronouns in simple sentences.

The subject of a sentence is the person or thing doing something. The object is the person or thing to whom or for whom the thing is done. Often the subjects or objects are pronouns.

Look at the following example:

José gave his book to Maria.

<u>He</u> gave his book to <u>her</u>.

Here are the subject and object pronouns:

Subject Pronouns	Object Pronouns
I	me
you	you
he	him
she	her
it	it
we	us
they	them

A Make up answers to the questions. In your answers, replace the underlined words with object pronouns. The first one is done for you.

1. What did you ask <u>Robert</u>?

   I asked him to be quiet.

2. What did the teacher tell <u>the children</u>?

_____

3. What did those women ask <u>you and me</u>?

_____

4. What did Rajiv tell <u>his mother</u>?

_____

5. What did Mr. Adler ask <u>the waiter</u>?

_____

6. What did the driver do to the <u>lamp post</u>?

_____

B Circle the correct pronoun for each sentence. The first one is done for you.

1. John will meet (we / us) at the theater.

2. I have already played chess with (they / them).

3. (I / Me) get a lot of vitamin A.

4. Do you want (he / him) to leave now?

5. (She / Her) had a summer job at the bakery.

6. I'm going to take (they / them) to the airport.

7. Tell (he / him) to turn down the radio.

8. I had a long talk with (she / her) and her sister.

SKILL OBJECTIVE: Reviewing subject and object pronouns. Go over the grammar explanation in the box at the top of the page. Do Parts A and B together orally if you believe students will have difficulty with them. Otherwise assign the page as independent work.

Dear Dot

Dear Dot,
    I bought my girlfriend an expensive necklace for her birthday. She liked it, but she wouldn't accept it. She told me that her mother taught her not to accept such expensive presents from someone she was not engaged to. I am very disappointed. I want her to have this necklace, and I don't care about some silly rule of etiquette that says otherwise. Dot, does that old rule really matter anymore?

                                    Diamond Jim

1. What did Jim buy his girlfriend for her birthday? _____

_____

2. Why didn't his girlfriend accept the gift? _____

_____

3. How does Jim feel about the situation? _____

_____

4. What does Jim want? _____

_____

5. What does the word *silly* mean in this letter? Circle the best answer.

   a. foolish   **b.** old   **c.** friendly   **d.** careful

6. What is your advice to Jim? Discuss your answer in class. Then take Dot's role and write a letter to Jim answering his question.

   _____ ,

   _____

   _____

   _____

   _____

   _____

                                    _____

SKILL OBJECTIVES: Reading for details; drawing conclusions; making judgments; writing a letter. Have students read the letter and answer questions 1–5 independently. Correct these as a class. Then have students discuss question 6 and write their letters. Ask several volunteers to read their letters, and have the class make suggestions for rephrasing, etc. As an additional option, have students write a paragraph about some of the rules of "etiquette" that were a part of their upbringing.

Unit 9 Something, Anything
Anything and Everything

Language Objective
Complete sentences with indefinite adjectives and pronouns.

Some and *any* are called indefinite adjectives because they refer to an amount or quantity that is not definite or specific. *Somebody, anybody, something,* and *anything* are called indefinite pronouns because they do not name or refer to definite or particular persons or things.

Complete each of the sentences by filling each blank with one of the following indefinite adjectives or pronouns: *some, any, somebody, anybody, something, anything.* The first one is done for you.

1. She doesn't have _____*any*_____ money in her bank account.

2. There are _____ students from China in my class.

3. I don't think _____ has seen her recently.

4. There aren't _____ students in my class from Russia.

5. Shhh! I think I hear _____ in the next room.

6. _____ ate my lunch!

7. May I have _____ more tea, please?

8. I wanted to borrow _____ money from her but she said that she didn't have

    _____ .

9. She never gives her poor cat _____ milk to drink.

10. The police asked me _____ questions but I didn't know _____ .

11. I didn't have _____ milk, so I went to the store to buy _____ .

12. I entered the room but I didn't see _____ so I left.

13. I thought I heard a noise in the next room but my wife didn't hear _____ .

14. It's my mother's birthday tomorrow, so I have to go out and buy her _____ .

15. There is _____ wrong with my bike.

16. Mr. Villalba never gives his wife _____ money.

17. The baby is hungry, so I'm giving her _____ to eat.

18. David didn't want _____ to eat.

19. _____ just telephoned you; he's going to call back later.

20. I have _____ to tell you.

SKILL OBJECTIVE: Using indefinite pronouns and adjectives. Teach/review the indefinite adjectives and pronouns asking, "Do you have any (some) questions?" ("No, I don't have *any* questions./Yes, I have *some* questions.") "Is there anybody (somebody) in the hall? Do I have anything (something) behind my back?" Note that negative statements use *any, anybody, anything,* and positive statements use *some, somebody,* and *something.* Questions can use either form. Do the first few items on this page as a class, then assign for independent written work.

I Just Ate!

The word *just* has several meanings. One meaning of *just* is "recently in the past." It is used with the past tense or the present perfect tense. "I just ate" and "I have just eaten" both mean "I finished eating a few minutes ago."

Use the word *just* in your answers to the questions below. The first two are done for you. Use them as models for the others.

1. Why is John upset?

   John is upset because his dog has just eaten part of the rug.

2. Why is Lisa happy?

   Lisa is happy because she just won $1000 in the lottery.

3. Why is Christina happy?

4. Why is Rolando upset?

5. Why is Mrs. Poleo mad?

6. Why is Alexis happy?

7. Why is Carla sad?

8. Why are Mr. and Mrs. Soto happy?

9. Why is Mr. Nguyen upset?

**SKILL OBJECTIVE: *Using *just* with present perfect and simple past.* Whisper to a student, "Write on the board." Then ask, "What did s(he) just do?" If needed, prompt answer, "She just wrote on the board." Direct another student to erase the board and ask, "What has he just done?" If needed, provide additional situations for oral practice. Go over the first two items together. Point out that either the simple past or the present perfect can be used. Assign as independent written work.

85

Why Did It Happen?

Language Objective
Match results and causes and write complex sentences using the conjunction <u>because</u>.

Often you have to explain to someone why something happened. In the exercise below, there are *results*—what actually happened— in Column 1 and *causes*—why the things happened—in Column 2.

A   Match the causes in Column 2 with the results in Column 1 by writing the letter of the cause next to the result. The first one is done for you.

Results		Causes
1. I lost my money	_q_	**a.** Thanksgiving was coming
2. They got wet	_____	**b.** the weather was cool and windy
3. He tripped	_____	**c.** it was so happy
4. We sank	_____	**d.** he was going out in the dark
5. The cat scratched itself	_____	**e.** I wanted to stay under water for twenty seconds
6. We said thank you	_____	**f.** he had no idea what it was
7. We bought a turkey	_____	**g.** they forgot to bring their umbrellas
8. I sent May a valentine	_____	**h.** they wanted the fight to be finished and forgotten
9. The dog wagged its tail	_____	**i.** it had fleas
10. Bob yawned	_____	**j.** there was no hook on our line
11. I zipped my jacket	_____	**k.** he didn't see the bumps in the rug
12. I took a deep breath	_____	**l.** there was no extra chair for her
13. We turned on the fan	_____	**m.** he didn't like the grade he got on his test
14. Tim got a flashlight	_____	**n.** someone bought us a gift
15. Bill frowned	_____	**o.** I'm in love with her
16. Mike guessed the answer	_____	**p.** it was a hot, sticky day
17. We put on masks and costumes	_____	**q.** there was a hole in my pocket
18. The boys shook hands	_____	**r.** he was tired and wanted to go
19. We didn't catch a fish	_____	**s.** there were holes in the bottom of the boat
20. The baby sat on my lap	_____	**t.** it was Halloween night

B   In your notebook, write ten of the sentences you have matched, joining them with the word *because*.

Example: I lost my money because there was a hole in my pocket.

SKILL OBJECTIVES: Determining cause and effect; writing sentences. Explain the directions to students and go over any new vocabulary. Do the first three items together, then assign the page as independent work.

Using Reference Books

A reference book is a book designed to provide information on one or more subjects. Dictionaries and encyclopedias are reference books. There are many other kinds of reference books, too. Some of these are described below. Look at the descriptions and use them to help you complete the page.

Almanac: a yearly publication that includes lists, charts and tables, and summaries of information in many unrelated fields.

Atlas: a collection of maps; atlases often also include population statistics.

Book of Quotations: a listing of well-known quotations from authors, politicians, and other famous people. The quotations are indexed to make them easy to find.

Facts on File: a bimonthly summary of major stories in more than fifty United States and foreign newspapers. Complete indexes make stories easy to locate.

Thesaurus: a book of synonyms and antonyms.

Readers' Guide to Periodical Literature: an author/subject index of articles and stories in a large number of magazines published in the United States. It comes out twice a month (once a month in certain months).

Now look at the topics below. Tell which of the reference books described above you might use to find more information about the subject. Include the dictionary and encyclopedia. The first one is done for you.

1. the height of Mount Shasta — *atlas (or almanac, encyclopedia)*

2. synonyms for the word *run* — _____

3. maps of the Central Plains states — _____

4. riots in Baghdad last year — _____

5. who wrote "To be or not to be …" — _____

6. the opposite of *careful* — _____

7. recent developments in bilingual education — _____

8. rainfall in Tokyo — _____

9. antonyms for the word *happy* — _____

10. source of "A penny saved is a penny earned." — _____

11. current population of Senegal — _____

12. a series of recent murders in New York City — _____

13. another word meaning *laugh* — _____

14. articles about track competition — _____

15. last month's elections in Honduras — _____

16. the origin and different meanings of *rich* — _____

17. all magazine articles by Sebastian Unger — _____

18. maps of all the countries of Europe — _____

19. brief biographies of the Presidents — _____

20. the origin and history of the metric system — _____

The Peopling of the Americas (1)

Language Objectives
Define vocabulary. Answer questions about a reading.

A Make sure you know the meaning of the following words, which are underlined in the article.

humans	Beringia	climate	Stone Age
inhabited	Ice Age	nomadic	civilizations

B Read the article quickly to get some general ideas about it. Then read it again more slowly to answer the questions.

From Asia to America

Humans are new to the Americas. Humans have inhabited the Earth for millions of years. But they have lived in the Americas for about 35,000 years. This is what some scientists think probably happened. The very first people to come to the Americas probably walked! They came from Asia over a land bridge called Beringia. This bridge stretched between Asia and Alaska. It was formed during the Ice Age. At this time, much of the earth's water was frozen. Ocean levels were much lower.

The earliest travelers to the Americas were hunter-gatherers. They followed herds of animals across Beringia. Or they came looking for new hunting or fishing grounds. Either way, it was a hostile new land covered with ice and snow.

Then, about 14,000 years ago, the climate began to change. It got warmer. The ice melted. Sea levels rose. The sea covered the land bridge between Asia and the Americas. As the land became easier to explore, people began to move. Over the next two or three thousand years, people moved through North America and Central America and into South America. Finding evidence of these early settlers isn't easy. They were nomadic. There were few permanent settlements. What evidence there is shows that people were well established in the Americas 11,000 years ago. These Stone Age people made tools from wood and chipped stone.

When the Europeans arrived in 1492, the Americas were sparsely settled. In fact, there were some amazing civilizations. In Central and South America, the Mayas, the Incas, and the Aztecs had built incredible cities. Many were bigger and more advanced than European cities at the time. In North America, tribes lived from the west coast to the east coast. Each tribe developed its own language and culture. This process took 10,000 years.

Scientists are studying the DNA of Asian and American people to find links between them. This science is very new. But it's beginning to show how closely related all people of the world are.

C Answer the following question. You may choose more than one answer.

Why did people come to the Americas from Asia?

a. They were hungry.

c. They were looking for new places to hunt.

b. They were adventurous.

d. They followed herds of animals.

(Go on to the next page.)

SKILL OBJECTIVES: Reading comprehension; inferring character traits; building vocabulary. Review the directions with the students. After the first reading, you may want to lead a discussion about the meaning of the highlighted vocabulary words. Encourage students to check and refine their definitions by using a dictionary. Display U.S. and world maps. Have students locate the places mentioned in the reading. *Extension Activity:* Help students outline the information in the second and third paragraphs: *I. The Ice Age* and *II. The Stone Age.*

D You can often guess something not stated in the text from the facts you read. Decide which of the answers best completes the sentence, and circle it.

The people who came across the land bridge probably

a. lived an easy life.

b. returned to Asia.

c. had a map to guide them.

d. did not realize they were the first people in the Americas.

E Use a word from the underlined vocabulary to complete each of these sentences.

1. No one lived in the building; it was not _____.

2. It was so cold I thought we were having a new _____.

3. We moved so often I got used to a _____ life.

4. The food was for dogs, not for _____.

5. The weather is what it's like outside today. The _____ is what it's like outside year after year.

F Number the statements in the order in which they happened. The number 1 is done for you.

_____ The climate got warmer.

_____ Some of the Earth's ice melted.

___1___ About 35,000 years ago Asian hunter-gatherers walked to the Americas.

_____ Early people moved from north to south.

G Certain facts give clues to other things that happened. Look at the facts at the left. Find the statement at the right that goes with each clue, and write its letter in the blank. Use your dictionary for words you don't know.

1. All people's DNAs are similar in some ways. _____

2. There is no evidence of people in the Americas before 40,000 years ago. _____

3. Animals moved over the land bridge from Asia to the Americas. _____

4. There were few permanent settlements. _____

5. The climate got warmer. _____

6. Today we find stone tools buried deep in the Earth. _____

7. It was warmer in the south. _____

a. The ice melted.

b. Many people were nomads.

c. People moved from north to south.

d. There were probably no people in the Americas 40,000 years ago.

e. People long ago used stone tools.

f. Hunters followed the animals over the land bridge.

g. People may be more alike than they are different.

H Use an atlas to locate where the land bridge from Asia probably was. Draw a simple diagram of the continents of Asia and North and South America. Label the "bridge."

SKILL OBJECTIVES: Predicting outcomes; making inferences; sequencing; researching and writing a short report. *Part H:* The Mayas, the Incas, and the Aztecs were three civilizations that developed in Central and South America. Have students locate where these civilizations existed on a map, then choose one to research. Remind students to skim encyclopedia articles to find the section about the topic they are interested in, take notes, then individually or as a group, write a report.

It's Your Choice

Sometimes the present perfect tense is used to describe things that have a "present" meaning—things that are happening at the present time. Sometimes it is used with a "past" meaning, to describe things that are not happening at the present time but did happen in the past.

A Read the sentences below. Decide if the sentence has a present or a past meaning and write present or past in the blank. The first two are done for you.

1. _present_   I have been in the United States for two months. (I am here now.)

2. _past_   I have been to New York City twice. (I went there in the past.)

3. _____   Ramon has already seen that movie.

4. _____   You have worked at that store for three months.

5. _____   They have worked at many jobs.

6. _____   I have known Trang since 2001.

7. _____   I have read that book before.

8. _____   Michiko has had her driver's license since she was 16.

9. _____   He has had three operations on his knee.

10. _____   Lucienne has been teaching French for a long time.

11. _____   Spiro and Galina have recently graduated from college.

12. _____   They have studied English since last August.

B Complete each sentence with either the simple past or the present perfect tense of the verb in parentheses. The first two are done for you.

1. The company (sell) _has sold_ millions of pairs of jeans since it opened in 1935.

2. Our teacher (give) _gave_ us two tests last month!

3. When Robert was in France, he (see) _____ the movie *Amelie* three times.

4. Yoshiko (see) _____ the movie *Shrek* three times, and she plans to see it again.

5. The president of the United States (meet) _____ with the prime minister of Britain last week.

6. Natasha and Mikhail are taking guitar lessons. They (take) _____ them for a year.

SKILL OBJECTIVE: Contracting present perfect with present and past tenses. *Part A:* Explain the directions carefully and provide examples on the board if students have difficulty grasping the concept. Do all the items orally before having students write them if you believe students need this help. *Part B:* This is a review of the distinction between present perfect and past tenses. Do all items orally if you believe students still need this help.

Word Skills: Analogies

An *analogy* is a comparison between two sets of words. To complete an analogy, you must discover the relationship between the words in the first set, and then find a word that makes that same relationship with the first word in the other set. When you are completing the analogies on this page, think about the word skills you have already practiced in this book: synonyms, antonyms, homophones, and categories. These are some of the ways in which words in an analogy can relate to each other.

Look at the example below. Choose one of the four answers.

    big : little : : old : _____   small / tall / young / quiet

The correct answer is *young*. *Big* and *little* are antonyms, so you must find an antonym for *old*; the only one given is *young*. (Note: You read the analogy as "Big is to little as old is to young.")

Now complete each of the following analogies. Circle your answers.

1. breakfast : morning : : lunch : _____   meal / afternoon / dinner / eat

2. banana : yellow : : apple : _____   food / fruit / fresh / red

3. mouse : mice : : tooth : _____   mouth / white / animal / teeth

4. wall : clock : : wrist : _____   time / arm / watch / o'clock

5. to : too : : write : _____   wrote / paper / right / wrong

6. bottom : top : : cellar : _____   attic / basement / house / down

7. doctor : hospital : : professor : _____   subject / university / teacher / lawyer

8. blood : red : : sugar : _____   sweet / color / salt / white

9. up : down : : in : _____   into / on / out / from

10. glove : hand : : sock : _____   shoe / foot / leg / punch

11. winter : cold : : summer : _____   hot / season / sun / fever

12. ring : finger : : bracelet : _____   jewelry / arm / neck / chest

13. oak : tree : : rose : _____   woman / red / pink / flower

14. chauffeur : car : : pilot : _____   airplane / airport / fly / runway

15. fight : fought : : shoot : _____   gun / shot / enemy / west

16. bad : awful : : good : _____   better / wonderful / terrible / best

17. chemistry : science : : geometry : _____   mathematics / algebra / subject / Greek

18. film : movie : : cheap : _____   costly / store / sale / inexpensive

Two Careers

Look at the chart below. It gives you information about the careers of two people. Use this information to answer the questions.

Name	Place of Birth	Date of Birth	Came to U.S.A.	Address in U.S.A.	Degrees	College	Occupation Now
Amin Jabbour	Beirut, Lebanon	5/14/70	1/5/91	Quincy, MA 1991–1994	B.S. 1994 (civil engineering)	Northeastern University	Professor of Civil Engineering at the University of Texas 1996–
				Boston, MA 1994–1996	M.S. 1996 (civil engineering)	Massachusetts Institute of Technology (M.I.T)	
				Austin, TX 1996–			
Isabel Minton	Leeds, United Kingdom	5/3/65			B.A. 1987 (psychology)	University of Manchester	Psychologist in Bristol, U.K. 1994–
					M.A. 1991 (psychology)	University of London	
					Ph.D. 1994 (psychology)	University of London	

Note: MA = Massachusetts TX = Texas M.S. = Master of Science B.A. = Bachelor of Arts Ph.D. = Doctor of Philosophy

A **Answer the questions about Professor Jabbour in your notebook. Use complete sentences.**

1. Where was Professor Jabbour born?
2. When was he born?
3. Has he ever been to the U.S.A.?
4. When did he come to the U.S.A.?
5. Where did he live when he first came to the United States?
6. Where else has he lived?
7. How many times has he moved?
8. Where is he living now?
9. How long has he lived there?
10. How many degrees has he earned?
11. When did he get his B.S.? His M.S.?
12. After he got his B.S., how long did it take him to get his M.S.?
13. How many colleges has he attended?
14. What was his major field in college?
15. What is his occupation now?
16. How long has he been in the U.S.A.?
17. How old is he?

B **Write both the questions and answers about Dr. Minton's life. The first question is written for you. Use complete sentences and write them in your notebook.**

1. Where / born? _Where was she born?_
2. When / born?
3. How old / now?
4. Has / ever / be / U.S.A?
5. How many degrees / have?
6. When / get / B.A.? M.A.? Ph.D.?
7. Where / get / B.A.?
8. What / major / university?
9. How many universities / attend?
10. How old / get / Ph.D.?
11. What / occupation now?
12. Where / work?
13. How long / be / psychologist?
14. How long ago / get / B.A.?

SKILL OBJECTIVES: Interpreting a chart; reviewing verb tenses; answering and writing questions. Examine the chart as a class. If needed, explain the abbreviated dates and the meaning and pronunciation of the degree titles. Adjust the amount of preliminary discussion to the needs of your class, then assign the page as independent written work. *Extension Activities*: 1.) Have the class discuss ways in which Amin Jabbour and Isabel Minton are alike, and ways in which they are different. 2.) Have students write a short biography of Amin or Isabel based on the information in the chart.

Dear Dot

Language Objectives
Answer questions about a reading. Give advice. Agree or disagree with advice.

Dear Dot,

My girlfriend Karen has broken several dates with me recently. She calls me on the day of our date and says that she can't make it. Sometimes she explains, but most times she doesn't. Last week I drove to her apartment and I found a note on her door. It said that she was at her sister's house. I called the number she put in the note, but there was no answer. I have talked to Karen about this situation. She says that she still loves me, and that if I am patient, everything is going to be all right. I am trying to be patient, but I am getting tired of her canceling our dates. What's your opinion, Dot? What should I do?

Ted

1. What has happened to Ted recently? _____

_____

2. Does Karen explain when she breaks a date? _____

_____

3. What happened last week? _____

_____

4. Where did Karen say she was going to be? _____

_____

5. What is Ted getting tired of? _____

_____

6. What does the word *canceling* mean in this letter? Circle the best answer.

   a. calling about   **b.** calling for   **c.** calling off   **d.** calling in

7. What is your advice to Ted? Discuss your answer in class. Then write Ted a letter telling him what you think he should do and should not do.

   _____,

   _____

   _____

   _____

   _____

   _____

                                              _____

SKILL OBJECTIVES: Reading for details; drawing conclusions; making judgments; writing a letter. Have students read the letter and answer questions 1–6 independently. Correct these as a class. Then have students discuss question 7 and write their letters. Ask several volunteers to read their letters, and have the class make suggestions for rephrasing, etc. As an additional option, you may wish to have students write a letter from Karen to Ted explaining what she has been doing for the last six weeks and why she hasn't been able to see him.

Read the sentences and decide which of the following tenses to use.

- simple present
- present progressive
- simple past
- past progressive
- future
- present perfect

Then write the verb in the blank using the correct form of the tense you chose. The first one is done for you.

1. Roberto (be) _has been_ to New York three times. (present perfect)

2. Sometimes we (play) _____ cards on Friday nights.

3. Kathy and Mike are marrying in Chicago where they (live) _____ for six years.

4. The children (play) _____ outside when the fire started.

5. I (study) _____ French from 2000 to 2003.

6. The mail never (come) _____ on Sundays.

7. Trang (graduate) _____ from college next June.

8. We (stay) _____ at the Biltmore Hotel for a few days last year.

9. Paul Theroux (write) _____ more than twenty-five books since 1970.

10. When you (call) _____ me yesterday, I (type) _____ a term paper.

11. My grandmother (take) _____ two courses at the community college this semester.

12. Mae Ling (be) _____ ten on her next birthday.

13. It (rain) _____ now. It (rain) _____ for two days.

14. Listen! I think someone (knock) _____ at the door right now.

15. Ron and Jennifer usually (go) _____ to church on Sundays.

16. The Carlsson family (move) _____ three times since they arrived in this country.

17. A dog (bite) _____ John while he (wait) _____ for the bus last week.

18. How much was that sweater? It (cost) _____ $30.00.

19. Where is your sister? She (shop) _____.

20. The bus (come) _____ in a few minutes.

Word Skills: Categories

Language Objective
Demonstrate vocabulary knowledge by listing items that belong in a labeled category.

A good way to test your word knowledge is to complete categories of words. A category is a group of similar things, in this case words. After each category name below, write five words that belong in the category. Use any words that fit the category name. Use your dictionary or other books if you need to. The first one is done for you.

1. colors   <u>red</u>   <u>orange</u>   <u>green</u>   <u>blue</u>   <u>yellow</u>

2. clothing

3. vegetables

4. fruit

5. cities

6. states

7. countries

8. school subjects

9. large animals

10. small animals

11. months

12. sports

13. occupations

14. family members

15. machines

16. rooms in a house

17. kinds of buildings

18. weather words

19. motor vehicles

20. illnesses

SKILL OBJECTIVES: Classifying; reviewing vocabulary. After students have completed this page, ask volunteers to name the words they have listed after each category. Keep a tally or list of all the different items listed by members of the class for each category.

The Peopling of the Americas (2)

Language Objectives
Define vocabulary. Answer questions about a reading. Determine the correct sequence of events from a reading.

A Make sure you know the meaning of the following words, which are underlined in the article.

Vikings	explore	mission	rugged
culture	colonize	Pilgrims	conquered

B Read the article quickly to get some general ideas about it. Then read it again more slowly to answer the questions.

The first Europeans to reach America were the Vikings. They built several settlements in Newfoundland over 1,000 years ago. They didn't stay long and their culture did not spread.

Christopher Columbus sailed from Spain and arrived in the New World in 1492. He landed on a Caribbean island he named Hispaniola. News of his landing created excitement in Europe. Spaniards set sail to find riches, explore, and colonize. Pedro Menendez de Aviles established the first permanent city in North America in 1565. It was called St. Augustine and is in the state of Florida. Spaniards also began to explore what is now California on the West Coast. In 1542, Juan Cabrillo Rodriguez led a group of sailors up the coast from Mexico. They stopped briefly but didn't stay. About 200 years later, the Spanish established permanent settlements in California. In 1769 Father Junipero Serra and other priests started the first mission in San Diego.

The English also came to explore and settle this distant land. In 1584, Sir Walter Raleigh established a settlement on Roanoke Island off the coast of what is now North Carolina. Virginia Dare, the first English child born in the New World, was born there. But this settlement disappeared. No one knows what happened to it or its people. It's still a great mystery. The first permanent English settlement was Jamestown, Virginia, which was founded in 1607. In 1620, the *Mayflower* landed 300 miles north of Jamestown at Plymouth, Massachusetts. The people were called Pilgrims. They left England to seek religious freedom. The people in Jamestown and Plymouth were not used to living in such rugged conditions. They would not have survived if it were not for the help of Native Americans.

Other early settlers were the Dutch. The Dutch bought the island of Manhattan from Native Americans in 1626. Peter Minuit began building the fort of New Amsterdam. This spot was eventually conquered by the British and renamed New York. New York is now the largest city in the United States.

After the success of these first settlements, Europeans of all nationalities flocked to the New World.

C Think carefully and answer the following question. You may choose more than one answer.

Why did the first Europeans come to the New World?

a. They wanted to explore.

c. They wanted to find riches.

b. They wanted religious freedom.

d. They were curious.

(Go on to the next page.)

SKILL OBJECTIVES: Reading comprehension; drawing conclusions; building vocabulary. Review the directions with the students. After the first reading, you may want to lead a discussion about the meaning of the highlighted vocabulary words. Encourage students to check and refine their definitions by using a dictionary. Display a U.S. and world map. Have students locate the places mentioned in the reading.

D **What is this article mostly about?**
Circle your answer.

    a. the first English settlements in America

    b. the first European settlements in America

    c. how the Spanish explorers came to America

    d. why the Dutch came to Manhattan

The Landing of the Pilgrims

E **Use a word from the underlined vocabulary to complete each of these sentences.**

    1. The winter last year was so _____ we missed five weeks of school.

    2. The champion tennis player _____ all of her opponents.

    3. Lee wanted to _____ all the stores for the best prices.

    4. Dave's _____ in life was to make everyone laugh.

    5. In our _____ we shake hands to say hello.

F **Number the statements in the order in which they happened in the article. The number 1 is done for you.**

    _____ The first mission was in San Diego in 1769.

    ___1___ The first Europeans in America were Vikings.

    _____ Sir Walter Raleigh started a settlement in North Carolina.

    _____ The *Mayflower* landed in Massachusetts.

    _____ People from all over the world came to America.

    _____ Christopher Columbus came in 1492.

    _____ The Dutch settlement was made in Manhattan.

    _____ St. Augustine was settled in 1565.

G **Draw a line from each quotation at the left to the name of the most likely speaker.**

    1. "Look men! I see land ahead. The *Santa Maria* has arrived."

    2. "Now we can worship in freedom."

    3. "There is no use in staying here. Let's go!"

    4. "The Dutch will have the best harbor in America."

    5. "This will be the first settlement in this land of beautiful flowers—Florida!"

    a. Peter Minuit

    b. A Pilgrim

    c. Christopher Columbus

    d. The Viking leader

    e. Pedro Menendez de Aviles

SKILL OBJECTIVES: Identifying main idea; building vocabulary; sequencing; making inferences. Assign the page as independent written work. Correct and discuss as a class.

97

Crossword Puzzle

Write the words in the right places. Numbers 1 Across and
1 Down are done for you.

Across

1. what they did at the beach
4. battled
6. operated the car
7. what they did with the milk
10. kept out of sight
11. looked at or watched
12. I _____, I saw, I conquered.
13. didn't win
15. what the wind did
17. discovered
19. what the thief did
20. what the bicyclist did
21. mailed the letter
22. received
23. listened
26. constructed
28. said

Down

1. what the singers did
2. she _____ her bed
3. smashed the glass
4. what the pilot did
5. same as 23 across
8. was aware of
9. donated
10. She _____ the baby in her arms.
12. selected
14. wondered
15. She _____ home the bacon.
16. He _____ his new suit.
18. didn't give away
19. didn't stand
24. what the diners did
25. He _____ his homework.
26. what the mad dog did
27. what the front person did

(Answers are on page 117.)

SKILL OBJECTIVE: Reviewing the past tense of irregular verbs. Solve the first across and down clues as a class. Be sure students
understand how to fill in a crossword puzzle. Students may work on this puzzle individually or in pairs. Students can check their
spelling by referring to the verb list on page 114.

High Hopes

Language Objective
Read for details to answer and write questions.

A Read the story about Jean. Then answer the questions.
Use complete sentences. The first one is done for you.

Jean left his home in Haiti when he was 17. He had an aunt in the United States. She gave him a place to live and a job. Jean works in his aunt's grocery store in a Haitian neighborhood. Jean likes working there. He can study when it isn't busy, or when he has a break. Jean is going to night school. He wants to finish college so he can get a different kind of job. He has been studying engineering for two years. Jean wants to design machines. He's interested in machines that generate power. Jean knows it will take him some time to finish his studies. But he has high hopes for making a better life for himself.

1. How old was Jean when he left home? _He was 17 years old._

2. Where did Jean go? _____

3. Who has he been living with? _____

4. Where has he been working? _____

5. What does he do besides work? _____

6. Why does he want to finish college? _____

7. How long has he been studying? _____

8. What does he want to design? _____

9. What kind of machines is he interested in? _____

10. Is Jean hopeful about the future? _____

B Read the story about Juan. In your notebook, write questions like the ones about Jean.
Then write answers to the questions. You may wish to exchange notebooks with a
partner and answer each other's questions.

In 1988, just a few weeks before his 15th birthday, the word came. Juan could leave Cuba. But his family would have to stay behind. Juan wanted to escape the island. But he did not want to leave his family. Fortunately, he did not have to make the choice. His family made it for him. They took him to the airport. He clutched a small bag as they kissed him good-bye. There were many sad tears as Juan got on the plane. Would he ever see his family again? He took one last look and memorized their faces.

Juan has been homesick, but his heart is filled with high hopes for the future.

SKILL OBJECTIVES: Reading for details; reviewing verb tenses; writing and answering questions. Assign this page as
independent written work.

Stormy Weather

A Make sure you know the meaning of the following important words, which are underlined in the article.

dangerous	sleet	snowdrifts	tornado
meteorologists	hailstones	damage	severe
predict	blizzard	cloudburst	hurricane

B Read the article quickly to get some general ideas about it. Then read it again more slowly to answer the questions.

There's a saying in New England: "If you don't like the weather, wait a few minutes!" Imagine how boring it would be if the weather never changed. Weather makes life interesting, exciting, and even <u>dangerous</u>. People who study the weather are called <u>meteorologists</u>. They study and <u>predict</u> the weather. They tell us when the weather is going to be beautiful, or when the weather looks bad.

Cold temperatures cause all kinds of bad weather. Rain that freezes as it falls is <u>sleet</u>. Sleet storms make traveling slippery and dangerous. Hailstorms can be as bad or worse. Balls of frozen water, or <u>hailstones</u>, form high in the sky and then fall to the ground. The largest hailstones recorded were about 6.5 inches across. Hailstorms can ruin crops, break windows, dent cars, rip through roofs, and even kill people. A <u>blizzard</u> is a snowstorm with strong winds. It is dangerous to drive in a blizzard. Sometimes people become stranded on the highways. If enough snow falls and blows around, <u>snowdrifts</u> can trap people in their houses, too. Blizzards can knock down power lines and trees, and do serious damage. The Blizzard of 1978 did over $1 billion worth of <u>damage</u> to the New England states.

In warmer temperatures, there are other forms of bad weather. During a <u>cloudburst</u>, a huge amount of rain falls in a short period of time. The record for a cloudburst is 1.8 inches of rain in one minute on the island of Guadalupe in the Caribbean. Cloudbursts can cause crop damage, flooding, and loss of life.

A <u>tornado</u> is a <u>severe</u> kind of bad weather. A tornado is a whirling windstorm. The area that is affected by a tornado can be large or small. And a tornado can last a long or short time. But the damage is almost always devastating. Tornadoes can rip up trees, toss cars like toys, and destroy houses. On May 2, 1999, the largest tornado ever recorded in the United States hit Oklahoma. It was 5,250 feet in diameter. About seventy tornadoes hit Oklahoma that same day, killing forty people and causing $1.2 billion worth of damage.

The most dangerous weather form is a <u>hurricane</u>. A hurricane is a huge windstorm with lots of rain and strong winds. It can cover hundreds of square miles and can damage large areas. Most hurricanes occur in the summer. One of the worst hurricanes in recent history was Hurricane Andrew. This 1992 storm lasted twelve days and caused $25 billion worth of damage. To date, it is the most expensive storm in U.S. history.

C Think carefully and answer the following question.

According to the reading, what condition does not occur during a hurricane?

a. rain

c. snow

b. strong winds

d. damage

(Go on to the next page.)

SKILL OBJECTIVES: Reading comprehension; building vocabulary. Review the directions with the students. After the first reading, you may want to lead a discussion about the meaning of the underlined vocabulary words. Encourage students to check and refine their definitions by using a dictionary.

D Circle the answer that best completes the sentence.

A hurricane is different from a tornado because

   a. it causes hail.

   b. of its size.

   c. it causes damage.

   d. it happens on the East Coast.

E Use a word from the underlined vocabulary to complete each of these sentences.

   1. Playing with firecrackers is very _____.

   2. I can't _____ when I'll be going to New York again.

   3. The flood caused major _____ to the town center.

   4. Several _____ work at this television station.

   5. My headache was so _____, I had to sit down.

F Write answers to these questions in your notebook.

   1. What is a meteorologist?

   2. What is a hurricane?

   3. What is a tornado?

   4. Where was the biggest tornado recorded?

   5. What was the worst storm in U.S. history?

   6. What is a blizzard?

   7. What is a cloudburst?

   8. What is a snowdrift?

   9. What is hail?

   10. What is sleet?

G Weather maps are issued by the National Weather Service every day. They show the weather in different parts of the country. This map shows the mid-continental United States one February day. Look at the key at the top of the map and answer these questions.

   1. What is the weather like in the Northeast? _____

   2. What is the weather like in the Southwest? _____

   3. Where is it snowing? _____

   4. What is the coldest temperature on the map? _____

   5. What is the warmest temperature on the map? _____

   The Forecast For 7 a.m. EST
   Thursday, February 17
   ● Low Temperatures
   Rain ▨ Snow ▧
   Showers ▥ Flurries ✱✱

   National Weather Service
   NOAA US Dept of Commerce

H Use an encyclopedia to find out what the other symbols on the weather map mean. Write a paragraph in your notebook to tell about the most interesting weather you've ever experienced.

SKILL OBJECTIVES: Reading for details; building vocabulary; drawing conclusions; interpreting and writing about a weather map.
Assign Parts C–F as independent work. Display a map with state names to help students answer question G-3. If you wish, do Part G as a class. Explain "isotherms," the lines connecting points of equal temperature, and the symbols for high and low pressure areas and warm and cold fronts. *Extensions:* Collect weather maps from newspapers, listen to TV weather reports, and if possible, call local toll-free weather information.

Dear Dot

Dear Dot,
    My husband Jack is teaching our daughters to work with tools and fix things around the house— even the car. He says that nowadays girls have to be able to do things for themselves. I don't know how to fix the car or a sink or anything, for that matter, and to tell the truth, I really don't want to know. The girls seem to like doing the work, but I'm not sure if it is such a good idea. The other day I found them in the attic, trying to fix an old television set. I'm afraid that they could hurt themselves. What do you think? Should I put a stop to all this?

                                        Old-Fashioned Mother

1. What is Jack doing for his daughters? _____

_____

2. Why is he doing this? _____

_____

3. How do the girls feel about their lessons? _____

_____

4. What is Old-Fashioned Mother afraid of? _____

_____

5. What does the word *seem* mean in this letter? Circle your answer.

    a. appear   **b.** need   **c.** looked   **d.** want

6. What do you think Old-Fashioned Mother should do? Discuss your answer in class. Then take Dot's role and write Old-Fashioned a letter giving her your advice.

    _____ ,

_____

_____

_____

_____

_____

_____

                                          _____

SKILL OBJECTIVES: Reading for details; drawing conclusions; making judgments; writing a letter. Have students read the letter and answer questions 1–5 independently. Correct these as a class. Then have students discuss question 6 and write their letters. Have several volunteers read their letters, and have the class make suggestions for rephrasing, etc. As an additional option, have each student write about something he or she does well—making scrambled eggs, changing a tire, painting a room, for example. The student should write clear directions for the activity, as if they were for someone who has never done the activity before.

Language Objectives
Write the comparative form of adjectives. Complete sentences using the comparative form of adjectives.

Look at the rules for writing the comparative form of adjectives.

Rule 1: For one-syllable adjectives: add *-er* and *than.*

| large | larger than | New York is *larger than* Chicago. |
| fast | faster than | A car is *faster than* a bicycle. |

Rule 2: For two-syllable adjectives that end in *y:* change *y* to *i*, add *-er* and *than.*

| easy | easier than | Math is *easier than* physics. |
| pretty | prettier than | Your dress is *prettier than* mine. |

Rule 3: For other adjectives of two or more syllables: use *more* _____ *than.*

| famous | more famous than | Tiger Woods is *more famous than* Sergio Garcia. |
| expensive | more expensive than | Steak is *more expensive than* chicken. |

Rule 4: Irregular adjectives

| good | better than | Tea is *better than* coffee, I think. |
| bad | worse than | My English is *worse than* yours. |

A **Add *-er* or *more* _____ *than* to the following words. Use the rules to help you. The first two are done for you.**

1. big _____bigger than_____
2. pretty _____prettier than_____
3. good _____
4. boring _____
5. small _____
6. important _____
7. nice _____
8. valuable _____

9. warm _____
10. intelligent _____
11. popular _____
12. noisy _____
13. great _____
14. smart _____
15. expensive _____
16. poor _____

B **Write the correct form of the comparative in the sentences below. The first one is done for you.**

1. The Nile River is (long) _____longer than_____ the Amazon River.
2. People are (intelligent) _____ animals.
3. Florida is (sunny) _____ Michigan.
4. Boston is (small) _____ New York City.
5. I think that history is (interesting) _____ algebra.
6. Chicago is (cold) _____ Miami.
7. A Honda Civic is (economical) _____ an SUV.
8. A Toyota is (cheap) _____ a Mercedes.
9. Dogs are (friendly) _____ cats.
10. I think that chicken is (good) _____ fish.

SKILL OBJECTIVE: Learning rules for forming comparatives. Review the rules with the class and write additional examples on the board. *Part A:* Show how the two examples follow rules 1 and 2. Then assign the rest of Part A. *Part B:* Be sure students understand the use of the adjective in parentheses: *(long)* is the word that is to be written in the comparative form. Assign Part B for independent work.

Superlatives with Adjectives

Language Objectives
Write the superlative form of adjectives. Complete sentences using the superlative form of adjectives.

Look at the rules for writing the superlative form of adjectives.

Rule 1: For one-syllable adjectives, use *the* + *-est*.

| large | the largest | Tokyo is *the largest* city in the world. |
| tall | the tallest | The Taipei 101 Tower is *the tallest* building. |

Rule 2: For two-syllable adjectives that end in *y*: change *y* to *i* and add *-est*.

| pretty | the prettiest | I think Sue is *the prettiest* girl in the class. |
| funny | the funniest | José is *the funniest* person I know. |

Rule 3: For two or more syllables: use *the most* _____.

| beautiful | the most beautiful | I think Paris is *the most beautiful* city. |
| handsome | the most handsome | Max is *the most handsome* boy in our club. |

Rule 4: Irregular adjectives

| good | the best | Kim is *the best* student in my class. |
| bad | the worst | "Jim's Diner" is *the worst* restaurant in town. |

A Add *-est* or *the most* _____ to the following words. Use the rules to help you. The first two are done for you.

1. famous   *the most famous*
2. large   *the largest*
3. rich   _____
4. heavy   _____
5. honest   _____
6. modern   _____
7. strong   _____
8. powerful   _____

9. bad   _____
10. lazy   _____
11. economical   _____
12. exciting   _____
13. ugly   _____
14. straight   _____
15. cheap   _____
16. interesting   _____

B Write the correct form of the superlative in the sentences below. The first one is done for you.

1. Mt. Everest is (high) _____*the highest*_____ mountain in the world.

2. Queen Elizabeth II is probably (rich) _____ woman in the world.

3. John F. Kennedy was (young) _____ president of the United States.

4. *The New York Times* is (important) _____ newspaper in New York.

5. Picasso's paintings are (expensive) _____ paintings in the world.

6. Tiger Woods is (famous) _____ golf player in the United States.

7. (old) _____ university in the world is in Morocco.

8. Many Americans think that Abraham Lincoln was (great) _____ U.S. president.

SKILL OBJECTIVE: Learning rules for forming superlatives. Review the rules with the class and write additional examples on the board. *Part A:* Show how the two examples follow rules 3 and 1. Then assign the rest of Part A. *Part B:* Be sure students understand how to complete the sentences, then assign Part B as independent written work.

Fact or Opinion?

You remember that a fact is a generally accepted statement of truth that can be checked in a dictionary, encyclopedia, or other reference book. An opinion, on the other hand, expresses a personal feeling, idea, or point of view.

Read the following statements. Decide if each is a fact or an opinion. If it is a fact, circle the *F*. If it is an opinion, circle the *O*.

1. The United States is larger than Cuba.	F O
2. Summer is the best season of the year.	F O
3. California is prettier than New York.	F O
4. St. Augustine is the oldest city on the United States mainland.	F O
5. The Rocky Mountains are higher than the Appalachians.	F O
6. Movies are more interesting than television programs.	F O
7. Spanish is more difficult to learn than French.	F O
8. Puppies are the cutest of all baby animals.	F O
9. Alaska is the largest of the fifty states.	F O
10. The Pacific Ocean is the largest of the four oceans.	F O
11. Apples are more delicious than oranges.	F O
12. Fresh fruit is more nutritious than potato chips.	F O
13. The Nile is the longest river in the world.	F O
14. Paris is the most interesting city in Europe.	F O
15. The moon is the Earth's closest neighbor in the sky.	F O
16. China has the largest population of any country in the world.	F O
17. Hurricanes occur most often in the summer.	F O
18. George Washington was the best U.S. president.	F O
19. Cancer is the worst disease that a person can have.	F O
20. Christopher Columbus crossed the ocean in 1492.	F O
21. The atom is a very small particle of matter.	F O
22. The Declaration of Independence is a radical document.	F O
23. Liver is richer in vitamin B than eggs.	F O
24. The sun is farther away from the Earth than is Mars.	F O
25. The American colonists were right to revolt against the British.	F O
26. Thomas Edison was the greatest American inventor.	F O
27. Train travel is more comfortable than plane travel.	F O
28. There is no life as we know it on the moon.	F O
29. Democracy is the best form of government.	F O
30. Gold is more expensive than silver.	F O

SKILL OBJECTIVE: Discriminating between fact and opinion. Read the introductory paragraph aloud. Complete and discuss the first few items as a class, then assign the page as independent work.

The U.S. Government

A Before you read the article, look at the Vocabulary Preview. Be sure that you know the meaning of each word. Use the dictionary. Some words have more than one meaning. The way the word is used in the story will help you decide the meaning you want. Write down the meanings of the words you are not sure of.

Vocabulary Preview

government	_____	representatives	_____
fair	_____	voters	_____
efficient	_____	elect	_____
power	_____	president	_____
branches (of government)	_____	vice president	_____
responsibilities	_____	courts	_____
laws	_____	protect	_____
follow	_____	rights	_____

B Now read the article. Use the dictionary if there are other words that you are not sure about. Notice that the words from the Vocabulary Preview are underlined.

The Constitution of the United States is the plan for the American government. Important American leaders, including George Washington, James Madison, Alexander Hamilton, and Benjamin Franklin, wrote the Constitution in 1787. The writers wanted to build a fair and efficient government for the new nation. They wanted to be sure that no one person or group of people held all the power. So, they planned a government with three branches, or three separate parts. They divided the powers and responsibilities of government between these three branches.

The first branch of the United States government is the *legislative* branch. This is the branch that makes the laws. The second branch is the *executive branch*. This is the branch that carries out the laws. The third branch is the *judicial branch*. This is the branch that tells what the laws mean. It also makes sure that people follow the laws.

In the United States government, the legislative branch is the Congress. There are two parts of Congress, the Senate and the House of Representatives. The men and women in the Senate are called senators. American voters choose them. Senators serve for six years. There are two senators for each state in the United States. There are 50 states, so this means that there are 100 senators.

The men and women in the House of Representatives are called representatives. American voters elect them also. They serve as representatives for two years. States with many people have many representatives. States with few people have few representatives. There are about five times more representatives than senators in Congress.

The president and vice president are in the executive branch. They have many thousands of people to help them carry out the laws and run the government. Americans elect the president and vice president every four years.

The judicial branch is the Supreme Court and other courts. The courts decide what a law means and if it follows the Constitution or not. All laws have to follow the Constitution. The courts make sure that people follow the laws. In this way they protect the rights of all Americans.

SKILL OBJECTIVES: Reading comprehension; building vocabulary. Allow time for students to look up vocabulary words in the dictionary and choose the appropriate definition. Review the definitions together. If you wish, read the selection aloud before asking students to read it silently. *Extension Activity:* After completing the reading, ask students, "Who is the president of the U.S.? Who is the vice president? Are they Democrats or Republicans? When is the next election? Who are the state's senators? Who is the local representative?"

Vacation Time

Travel is big business. Hotels, airlines, and travel agents advertise in newspapers and magazines to attract visitors to vacation spots. Here are three advertisements. Complete them with appropriate words. The first one is done for you. Use comparatives in the second advertisement and superlatives in the third.

COME TO BEAUTIFUL BERMUDA!

The beaches are ___clean___ and ___white___ !

The weather is ___warm___ and ___sunny___ !

The people are ___friendly___ !

The hotels are ___modern___ !

The food is ___delicious___ !

The rooms are ___exciting___ and ___cheap___ !

Yes, come to Bermuda, and you'll have a ___great___ time!

ONLY $799!
HOTEL & AIR FARE

COME TO ROMANTIC ARUBA!

The beaches are ___cleaner___ and ___whiter___ !

The weather is _____ and _____ !

The people are _____ !

The hotels are _____ !

The food is _____ !

The rooms are _____ and _____ !

Yes, come to Aruba, and you'll have a _____ time!

ONLY $899!
HOTEL & AIR FARE

COME TO SUPER ST. THOMAS!

The beaches are ___the cleanest___ and ___whitest___ !

The weather is _____ and _____ !

The people are _____ !

The hotels are _____ !

The food is _____ !

The rooms are _____ and _____ !

Yes, come to St. Thomas and you'll have _____ time!

ONLY $999!
HOTEL & AIR FARE

SKILL OBJECTIVE: **Using comparatives and superlatives.** Review the directions with the class, then assign this page as independent work.

107

Vacation Deals

Words with more than two syllables usually do not use *-er* and *-est* to form the comparative and superlative. Instead, they use the words *more* and *the most*. For example, the comparative of *exciting* is *more exciting*. The superlative is *the most exciting*.

Use this rule to write advertisements for these three vacation packages. Use comparatives and superlatives in your ad.

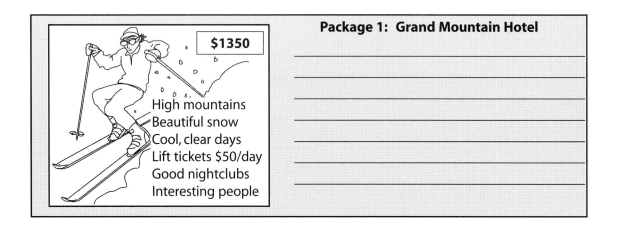

Package 1: Grand Mountain Hotel

_____

_____

_____

_____

_____

_____

$1350

High mountains
Beautiful snow
Cool, clear days
Lift tickets $50/day
Good nightclubs
Interesting people

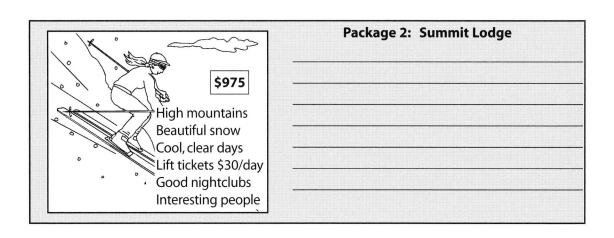

Package 2: Summit Lodge

$975

High mountains
Beautiful snow
Cool, clear days
Lift tickets $30/day
Good nightclubs
Interesting people

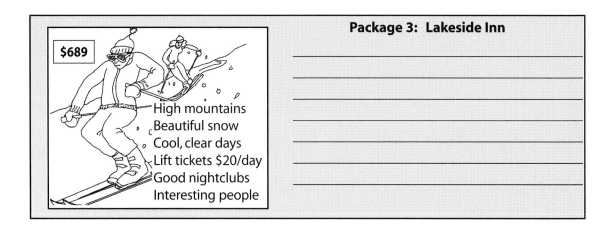

Package 3: Lakeside Inn

$689

High mountains
Beautiful snow
Cool, clear days
Lift tickets $20/day
Good nightclubs
Interesting people

SKILL OBJECTIVES: Constructing comparatives and superlatives; using *more* and *the most*. Write the first travel ad as a class, using the information in the ad and following the style set on page 107. You may wish to have the class compose the other two ads orally before assigning the page as independent written work. *Extension Activity:* Have students write a travel ad, using superlatives to describe their school, town, favorite store, or native country.

Tour the Sunshine State

Read the article.

Florida is called the Sunshine State. It has a warm climate and lots of sunshine. It's the state with the longest ocean coastline. Winter is Florida's biggest tourist season. But it doesn't matter when you visit Florida, there's something to do 365 days a year.

St. Augustine, Florida, is the oldest city in the United States. It was founded by the Spanish in 1565. It's a great place to shop or enjoy the charm of Spanish architecture.

At Cape Canaveral in southern Florida, visitors can visit the Kennedy Space Center. Learn about the NASA space program, meet an astronaut, or watch a rocket launch.

Orlando, Florida, is one of the most popular tourist destinations in the world. It has many theme parks and resorts. The largest is Disney World.

Tampa's history is revealed in the historic district of Ybor City. Visitors can see a restored tobacco factory, stroll through the shops, or eat lunch. There's definitely a Cuban flare in this old part of town. Many people from Cuba came to live in this part of Florida.

Heading east and south is Miami, Florida's largest city. It's home to three major league sports teams: the Miami Dolphins, the Miami Heat, and the Florida Marlins. Miami Beach is lined with hundreds of hotels facing the warm, turquoise water of the Atlantic Ocean. South Beach is a popular spot for young and old alike. There are lots of restaurants and beautiful old Art Deco buildings that have been recently restored.

Florida has something for everyone. No wonder Florida is so popular!

A Read the statements below. If the statement is true, write *T*. If the statement is false, write *F*. If the article doesn't give you enough information to know if the statement is true or false, write *?*. The first two are done for you.

1. Florida is called the Show Me State. _____F_____

2. Many retired people live in Florida. _____?_____

3. Florida is sunny. _____

4. St. Augustine was founded by the Pilgrims. _____

5. St. Augustine was founded in 1565. _____

6. Cape Canaveral is in central Florida. _____

7. Rockets launch from the Kennedy Space Center. _____

8. Orlando is a popular tourist destination. _____

9. About 40,000 tourists a day visit Disney World. _____

10. Sea World has a dolphin show. _____

11. Ybor City is the old part of Tampa. _____

12. Miami has three major league sports teams. _____

13. Miami Beach is on the Atlantic Ocean. _____

14. South Beach has nightclubs. _____

B Write why you would like or not like to visit Florida in your notebook. If you live in Florida, what other state would you like to visit? Why?

SKILL OBJECTIVES: Reading for details; distinguishing between *true, false,* and *?*. *Part A:* Go over any new vocabulary, and find out what the students already know about Florida. Then have students read the article silently. Review the *T, F, ?* format; make sure students understand that the *?* response is used when the story doesn't give enough information to decide if the statement is true or false. (Some students may know from outside reading or personal experience that a statement is true or not true, but should still use the *?* response if this information is not in the story.)

Biggest, Largest, Longest!

A Make sure you know the meaning of the following important words which are underlined in the article.

whale	tons	tortoise	falcon	leopard
weigh	insect	ostrich	cheetah	penny

B Read the article quickly to get some general ideas about it. Then read it again more slowly to answer the questions.

Animal Champions

Zoologists, scientists who study animals, tell us the following facts about animals:

- The blue <u>whale</u> is the largest animal in the world. It can be 100 feet long and can <u>weigh</u> more than 100 <u>tons</u>.

- The longest <u>insect</u> is the walking stick. It can be up to 16 inches long.

- The largest fish is the shark. (Remember, a whale is not a fish; it is a mammal.) Sharks can be 45 feet long.

- The giant <u>tortoise</u> of South America has the longest life of any animal. These turtles can live to be 150 years old.

- The <u>ostrich</u> is the largest bird. Ostriches can be 8 feet tall. They can weigh 200 pounds.

- The fastest bird is the peregrine <u>falcon</u>. It can fly at speeds of more than 217 miles per hour.

- The fastest runner is the <u>cheetah</u>. This hunting <u>leopard</u> can run at speeds of 60 miles per hour.

- The tallest animal is the giraffe. Some giraffes are 19 feet tall.

- The anaconda is the longest and heaviest snake. It can be 37 feet long and weigh more than 250 pounds.

- Hummingbirds are the smallest birds. An adult hummingbird can weigh less than a <u>penny</u>.

- The largest animal on land is the African elephant. It can weigh more than 6 tons.

C Think carefully and answer the following question.

According to the article, which of the following could possibly live for more than a century?

a. cheetah   **b.** tortoise   **c.** anaconda snake   **d.** elephant

D Use a word from the underlined vocabulary to complete each of these sentences.

1. Those bricks _____ five pounds each.

2. I have a nickel, two dimes, a quarter, and a _____.

3. Troy is scared of any bug or _____.

4. The _____ is the largest animal in the sea.

5. Jean is as slow as an old _____.

(Go on to the next page.)

SKILL OBJECTIVES: Readings comprehension; restating information; building vocabulary. Review the directions with the students. After the first reading, you may want to lead a discussion about the meaning of the highlighted vocabulary words. Encourage students to check and refine their definitions by using a dictionary. Assign Part C as independent work.

E Decide whether each of these statements is true or false. If it is true, write *T*. If it is false, write *F*. If the article doesn't give you enough information to decide, write *?*.

1. A whale is larger than a shark. _____

2. A cheetah is faster than a peregrine falcon. _____

3. The most dangerous animal is the leopard. _____

4. An ostrich is taller than a giraffe. _____

5. A walking stick is a kind of bird. _____

6. The most intelligent animal is the whale. _____

7. An anaconda is a long and heavy insect. _____

8. Blue whales are larger than African elephants. _____

9. Zoologists are scientists who study animals. _____

10. The smallest animal on Earth is the hummingbird. _____

F Decide which class each of the following animals belongs to. Use the following classes: fish, amphibians, birds, reptiles, insects, and mammals. Use a dictionary or an encyclopedia if you are not sure. The first one is done for you.

1. eagle _____bird_____
2. monkey _____
3. shark _____
4. lion _____
5. snake _____
6. flea _____
7. eel _____
8. dragonfly _____
9. sea horse _____
10. minnow _____

11. frog _____
12. crocodile _____
13. grasshopper _____
14. starling _____
15. whale _____
16. auk _____
17. toad _____
18. bat _____
19. kiwi _____
20. salamander _____

G Find out about some other champions. Use an encyclopedia or the Internet if you need to. Use comparative and superlative forms of the adjective. The first one is done for you. Use it as a model for the others.

1. Long Rivers of the World

Amazon _____longer_____
Chang (Yangtze) _____long_____
Nile _____longest_____

2. Big States in the United States

California _____
Alaska _____
Texas _____

3. High Mountains of North America

McKinley _____
Orizaba (Citlaltepetl) _____
Logan _____

4. Large Lakes of North America

Michigan _____
Superior _____
Huron _____

SKILL OBJECTIVES: **Reading for details; drawing conclusions; classifying; building vocabulary.** Assign Parts C–E as independent written work. You may wish to identify and discuss the characteristics of the six animal classes (fish, amphibians, birds, reptiles, insects, and mammals) with the group before assigning Part F as independent work. A World Almanac would also be a good reference source for Part G.

Dear Dot

Dear Dot

Dear Dot,

    I am heartbroken. My boyfriend Rafael just broke up with me. He said that he has a new girlfriend. He says that she is prettier, funnier, nicer, and more intelligent than I am. He always told me that I was the prettiest, funniest, nicest, and most intelligent girl in the world. How could he change his mind like that? I still love him. He is the most attractive and interesting boy I have ever dated. What can I do to get him back?

Lorna

1. Why is Lorna heartbroken? _____

_____

2. How does Rafael describe his new girlfriend? _____

_____

3. What did he used to tell Lorna? _____

_____

4. How does Lorna describe Rafael? _____

_____

5. What does the word *attractive* mean in this letter? Circle your answer.

    a. bright   **b.** handsome   **c.** funny   **d.** frightening

6. What is your advice to Lorna? Discuss your answer in class, then write Dot's letter answering Lorna's question and telling her what you think she should do.

    _____,

_____

_____

_____

_____

_____

_____

_____

SKILL OBJECTIVES: Reading for details; drawing conclusions; making judgments; writing a letter. Have students read the letter and answer questions 1–5 independently. Correct these as a class. Then have students discuss question 6 and write their letters. Have several volunteers read their letters to the class and have others offer comments and suggestions for rephrasing, etc. As an additional option, ask students to write a description of something that is the best—the best place they ever lived, the best meal they ever ate, etc. Have them tell why it was the best and why it was better than other things of the same kind.

Verb Review: Past Tense (1)

Regular Verbs: Present and Past

a. End with *d* sound

agree / agreed	die / died	move / moved
allow / allowed	discover / discovered	order / ordered
amuse / amused	dry / dried	prepare / prepared
answer / answered	enjoy / enjoyed	remember / remembered
apply / applied	enter / entered	return / returned
arrive / arrived	fry / fried	save / saved
call / called	hurry / hurried	serve / served
carry / carried	learn / learned	stay / stayed
change / changed	listen / listened	study / studied
clean / cleaned	live / lived	travel / traveled
consider / considered	love / loved	try / tried
copy / copied	improve / improved	use / used
cry / cried	marry / married	worry / worried
describe / described		

b. End with *t* sound

accomplish/ accomplished	finish / finished	talk / talked
ask / asked	increase / increased	type / typed
bake / baked	look / looked	walk / walked
brush / brushed	pack / packed	wash / washed
chase / chased	pick up / picked up	watch / watched
cook / cooked	practice / practiced	wax / waxed
dress / dressed	miss / missed	work / worked

c. End with *id* sound

accept / accepted	decide / decided	paint / painted
attend / attended	demand / demanded	recommend / recommended
collect / collected	insist / insisted	start / started
complete / completed	invent / invented	suggest / suggested
correct / corrected	invite / invited	visit / visited
create / created	need / needed	want / wanted

Note: The past participles of regular verbs have the same form as the past tense.

Example: I study.   I studied yesterday.   I have studied all morning.

In your notebook, write twenty sentences using as many of the verbs on this list in the past tense as you can. Try to use two or three verbs in each sentence.

Example: He was amused, but he agreed with me and allowed me to go.

Verb Review: Past Tense (2)

Irregular Verbs: Present, Past, and Past Participle

am, is, are / was, were / been

begin / began / begun

bite / bit / bitten

bleed / bled / bled

blow / blew / blown

break / broke / broken

bring / brought / brought

build / built / built

buy / bought / bought

catch / caught / caught

choose / chose / chosen

come / came / come

cost / cost / cost

cut / cut / cut

do / did / did

drink / drank / drunk

drive / drove / driven

eat / ate / eaten

fall / fell / fallen

feed / fed / fed

feel / felt / felt

fight / fought / fought

find / found / found

fit / fitted (or fit) / fitted (or fit)

fly / flew / flown

freeze / froze / frozen

get / got / gotten

give / gave / given

go / went / gone

grow / grew / grown

have / had / had

hear / heard / heard

hide / hid / hid (or hidden)

hit / hit / hit

hold / held / held

keep / kept / kept

know / knew / known

lead / led / led

leave / left / left

lose / lost / lost

make / made / made

meet / met / met

pay / paid / paid

put / put / put

read / read / read

ride / rode / ridden

ring / rang / rung

rise / rose / risen

run / ran / run

say / said / said

see / saw / seen

sell / sold / sold

send / sent / sent

set / set / set

sew / sewed / sewn

shake / shook / shaken

shoot / shot / shot

show / showed / shown

sing / sang / sung

sit / sat / sat

sleep / slept / slept

speak / spoke / spoken

spend / spent / spent

split / split / split

stand / stood / stood

steal / stole / stolen

swim / swam / swum

take / took / taken

teach / taught / taught

tell / told / told

think / thought / thought

understand / understood/
    understood

wake / woke (or waked) /
    waked (or woken)

wear / wore / worn

win / won / won

write / wrote / written

In your notebook, write twenty sentences using as many of the verbs on this list in the past tense as you can. Try to use two or more verbs in each sentence. Then write twenty more sentences using the past participles of as many verbs as you can. Try to use different verbs from those you used in your past tense sentences.

SKILL OBJECTIVES: Reviewing irregular verb forms, simple past tense and past participles; writing creative sentences. Assign the writing exercise as optional independent written work.

End of Book Test: Completing Familiar Structures

Example: John is _____ than his sister.

    a. more old   **b.** (older)   **c.** more older   **d.** very older

1. Mary went to the library but her friends _____ go with her.

    a. weren't   **b.** aren't   **c.** don't   **d.** didn't

2. When did the plane arrive? It arrived _____.

    a. ten minutes ago   **b.** before ten minutes   **c.** in ten minutes   **d.** at ten minutes

3. Yesterday I _____ tired and stayed in bed.

    a. am   **b.** was   **c.** did   **d.** do

4. My friend _____ a new car.

    a. has   **b.** is having   **c.** have   **d.** is have

5. Cathy is _____ girl in the class.

    a. the most pretty   **b.** the prettiest   **c.** the more pretty   **d.** prettier than

6. I don't have much money but I have _____.

    a. little   **b.** a few   **c.** a little   **d.** few

7. Julio has been in the United States _____ 1998.

    a. for   **b.** until   **c.** after   **d.** since

8. How many times have you _____ the movie *Spider-Man 2*?

    a. see   **b.** saw   **c.** seeing   **d.** seen

9. I have _____ finished my homework.

    a. yet   **b.** been   **c.** already   **d.** until

10. Alexis is happy because he _____ a new car.

    a. has just bought   **b.** has bought yet   **c.** has been buying   **d.** has just buy

11. Bill _____ when I called him.

    a. was eating   **b.** ate   **c.** has eaten   **d.** is eating

12. Miami, Florida, is _____ than Boston.

    a. more warm   **b.** the warmest   **c.** warmer   **d.** more warmer

END OF BOOK TEST: Completing familiar structures. The following testing pages will help you evaluate each student's strengths and weaknesses and indicate his or her readiness to proceed to the next level of instruction. Review directions and examples with the class. *Part A:* Remind students to try each answer choice in the blank space to determine which choice is correct. Students should circle their answers.

115

13. The teacher told me _____ more often.

   a. to study   **b.** study   **c.** studying   **d.** studies

14. Robert cut _____ when he was shaving.

   a. him   **b.** his   **c.** himself   **d.** he

15. When Mr. Stevens was young, he _____ play football very well.

   a. could   **b.** can   **c.** was   **d.** did

16. Ilya likes _____.

   a. traveler   **b.** traveling   **c.** to traveling   **d.** traveled

17. There are _____ cookies in the kitchen.

   a. a little   **b.** a big   **c.** a few   **d.** a many

18. When Martha was young, she _____ wash the dishes every night.

   a. can   **b.** had to   **c.** was   **d.** have to

19. When I arrived, there wasn't _____ in the office.

   a. somebody   **b.** anybody   **c.** nobody   **d.** body

20. The police _____ the robber.

   a. catching   **b.** to catch   **c.** caught   **d.** were caught

21. Mrs. Ramic _____ at the bank since 1980.

   a. worked   **b.** working   **c.** works   **d.** has been working

22. Ellen can't talk on the telephone now because she _____ her hair.

   a. was washing   **b.** wash   **c.** is washing   **d.** washes

23. Janet can't drive a car because she _____ a license.

   a. hasn't had   **b.** doesn't have   **c.** don't have   **d.** didn't have

24. I bought these gloves _____.

   a. in two weeks   **b.** for two weeks   **c.** two weeks   **d.** two weeks ago

25. Dolores borrowed _____ books from the library.

   a. some   **b.** any   **c.** a little   **d.** much

END OF BOOK TEST: Completing familiar structures (continued). See annotation on page 115.

End of Book Test: Completing Familiar Structures (continued)

B Read each sentence. Write the correct form of the verb on the line.

Examples: **1.** Luz _____went_____ (go) to the bank yesterday.

2. Julio _____goes_____ (go) to the movies every day.

1. Tomorrow the hairdresser _____ (cut) my hair.

2. Last week George _____ (come) to class late.

3. My mother and father _____ (stay) at the Plaza Hotel now.

4. Isabel _____ (work) at the bank many years ago.

5. John _____ (be) in the United States for ten years.

6. The President of the United States _____ (make) $400,000 a year.

7. When I arrived home, my mother _____ (make) lunch.

8. Harry and Larry _____ (see) the movie *Toy Story* many times.

9. Paulo _____ (sleep) at present.

10. My father _____ (get) up at six o'clock every morning.

Answers to puzzle on page 98.

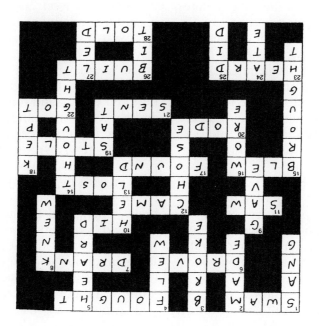

END OF BOOK TEST: Completing familiar structures (continued). Part *B:* Go over the directions and examples with the class before assigning the page as independent written work.

117

End of Book Test: Reading Comprehension

Read the article.

Sacajawea

A beautiful young girl named Sacajawea has her portrait on a United States coin. Who is she? This is her story.

Sacajawea was born in about 1785 in the northwestern mountains of what is now the United States. Her tribe was Shoshone. When she was about thirteen years old, Sacajawea was kidnapped by another tribe. This tribe, the Minnetaree, took Sacajawea from her home in the Rocky Mountains to the Central Plains.

Sacajawea lived with the Minnetaree for about four years. She learned their language. But she did not forget her first language and her Shoshone home.

When Sacajawea was seventeen a French trader, Toussaint Charbonneau, took her for his wife. So Sacajawea left the Minnetaree people and traveled with her husband. They went up and down the Missouri River, trading with tribes who lived there. Sacajawea must have learned some of her husband's language, French.

In the late fall of 1804, something happened that changed Sacajawea's life again. The President of the United States, Thomas Jefferson, sent two men to explore the western land along the Missouri River. The two men were Meriwether Lewis and William Clark. The men needed a guide and an interpreter. They hired Charbonneau to be their guide. Sacajawea would be their guide, too, and their interpreter. She could get information from the various tribes they would meet.

The journey would begin in spring. In February, Sacajawea had a baby. She named him Pompey. In a few weeks, after Pompey's birth, Sacajawea put him on her back and began the long trip that would take them over the mountains to the Pacific Ocean.

The young mother, a new baby, Charbonneau, Lewis and Clark, and their group of hired men would go by foot and by canoe. Along the way they would look for plants to eat. They would hunt animals for food. They would sleep on the ground in all kinds of weather. There were no bridges, so they waded across the rivers.

Along the way Sacajawea kept looking for signs that her Shoshone family were in the area. She knew that the explorers would pass through Shoshone hunting grounds. One happy day she did see her brother, Cameahwait. Imagine how they both felt to be able to see each other for the first time since Sacajawea's kidnapping. Her brother was a Shoshone chief now.

They were not together for very long. Sacajawea was not free to stay with her Shoshone family. The job of guiding and interpreting for the explorers was not finished. They left Cameahwait and went on across the mountains all the way to the Pacific Ocean.

Finally the northwest exploration and map-making trip was over. Lewis and Clark were anxious to return to report to President Jefferson. Sacajawea, her husband and baby were not going back east with Lewis and Clark. They would stay in the West and go back to trading.

On Saturday, August 17, 1806, Lewis and Clark paid Charbonneau five hundred dollars and thirty-three cents and gave him two canoes. They said goodbye to Sacajawea and to Pompey who was, Lewis wrote, "a beautiful, promising child of nineteen months." They never saw them again.

But Lewis and Clark did not forget the brave, bright, and beautiful Sacajawea who had been so important to their historic exploration. They told President Jefferson about her in their reports. They told spellbound audiences about their journey and always spoke of Sacajawea with appreciation.

(Go on to the next page.)

END OF BOOK TEST: **Reading comprehension.** Students should read the story several times before independently answering the comprehension questions on page 119. Encourage students to use context clues to guess the meanings of unfamiliar words. Dictionaries may also be used. The name of the heroine of this story is pronounced Sa kə jə wē 'ə.

A Answer the following questions. Use complete sentences.

1. Who kidnapped Sacajawea? _____

_____

2. Where did Lewis and Clark plan to go? _____

_____

3. Why did Charboneau and Sacajawea go with Lewis and Clark? _____

_____

4. How did Sacajawea carry her newborn baby on the long trip? _____

_____

5. How old was Pompey when the trip was over? _____

_____

B Number these statements in the correct chronological order.

_____ Charboneau took Sacajawea for a wife.

_____ Sacajawea found her Shoshone brother on the journey.

_____ Lewis and Clark hired Charboneau and Sacajawea.

_____ The Minnetaree kidnapped Sacajawea.

_____ Sacajawea helped the explorers through the Central Plains and the Rocky Mountains.

_____ The explorers went all the way to the Pacific Ocean.

_____ Sacajawea had a baby named Pompey.

C Draw a conclusion to complete the sentence. Circle your answer.

Lewis and Clark traveled through the West because

a. they were looking for gold.

b. they were looking for Sacajawea's family.

c. they were lost.

d. they were exploring western territory for President Thomas Jefferson.

D Write the letter of the quotation next to the speaker's name.

1. Sacajawea _____ | **a.** "My sister, how I have missed you all these years. I never expected to see you again."

2. Charboneau _____ | **b.** "It is your job to explore this new territory and report back to me as soon as possible."

3. Meriwether Lewis _____ | **c.** "I hope to return to the shining mountains, the land of my people."

4. Cameahwait _____ | **d.** "My partner and I need a guide to take us through the new land."

5. Thomas Jefferson _____ | **e.** "My wife will work hard and help me guide the explorers."

END OF BOOK TEST: Reading comprehension (reading for details, sequencing, drawing conclusions, making inferences). See annotation on page 118.

119

Index of Language Objectives